Scotland's Kings and Queens

ROYALTY AND THE REALM

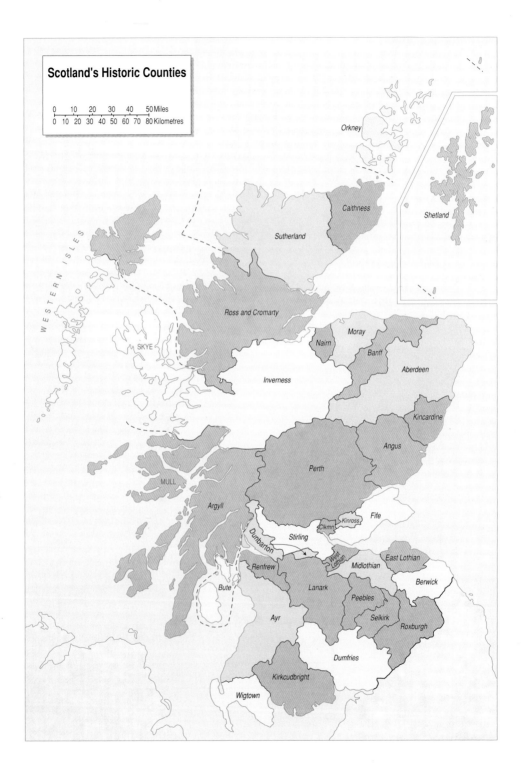

Scotland's Historic Counties

0   10   20   30   40   50 Miles
0 10 20 30 40 50 60 70 80 Kilometres

Orkney

Shetland

Caithness

Sutherland

W E S T E R N   I S L E S

Ross and Cromarty

Moray

Nairn

Banff

SKYE

Inverness

Aberdeen

Kincardine

Angus

MULL

Perth

Argyll

Fife

Kinross

Clkmn

Dunbarton

Stirling

West Lothian

East Lothian

Renfrew

Midlothian

Bute

Lanark

Berwick

Peebles

Ayr

Selkirk

Roxburgh

Dumfries

Kirkcudbright

Wigtown

DISCOVERING HISTORIC SCOTLAND

SCOTLAND'S KINGS AND QUEENS

ROYALTY AND THE REALM

RICHARD ORAM

SERIES EDITOR: ALEXANDRA SHEPHERD

HISTORIC SCOTLAND

EDINBURGH: THE STATIONERY OFFICE

ABOUT THE AUTHOR

Richard Oram is a freelance historian and specialist in Scottish medieval history. He gained his first degree and doctorate from St Andrews University and is now an honorary lecturer at the University of Aberdeen. He is Editor of the Birlinn series of Regional Historical Guides and is Secretary of the Baronial Research Group of the Scottish medievalists. He lives in Moray with his wife and two children.

ACKNOWLEDGEMENTS

The production of this book has involved me in long hours spent huddled over my PC keyboard, neglecting my wife and family. It is an experience to which they are becoming used, but I must still give my greatest thanks to my wife for her tolerance and support, and to Alasdair and Lauren, my children, for giving me the time to put this project to rest. To Lekky Shepherd must go my special thanks for her unstinting efforts as editor, her assistance in the shaping and fine-tuning of this volume going far beyond simple editorial duties. To Tom Mason at Centre Graphics for his skillful page make-up and to Mark D Dennis for the illustration on p. 8. There are many others whose ideas and advice have been incorporated into the pages which follow, to them all goes my deepest gratitude.

Cover illustrations show *front:* the Scottish Crown, symbol of monarchy (Historic Scotland) and an image of Mary Queen of Scots drawn from a gold ryal or £3 piece (Shepherd); *back:* Dumbarton Rock, citadel of one of the earliest Scottish Kingdoms (Oram) and the coronation of Robert the Bruce from a tableau in Edinburgh Castle (Historic Scotland).

First published 1997 by The Stationery Office Limited,
South Gyle Crescent, Edinburgh EH12 9EB

ISBN 0 11 495783 5

British Library Cataloguing in Publication Data

A catalogue record for this book
is available from the British Library

Applications for reproduction
should be made to The Stationery Office Limited

CONTENTS

FOREWORD

Scotland is a country where the imprint of history is still clearly visible in the landscape, in its houses, churches, farmsteads and settlements large and small. All these have coloured, and been coloured by, their setting in mountains or moorland, on fertile pasture or sandy shore, at loch-side or rivermouth. Of paramount importance has always been the all-encompassing influence of the sea for Scotland is set amidst the searoads of the Celtic provinces in the west and the Scandinavian regions to the north, the trading routes with the mainland of Europe to the east and the land and sea approaches to that dominant neighbour, England, in the south. Scotland's cultural history has thus been moulded by a mixture of influences, fluctuating in importance, absorbed and transformed in ways that are peculiarly Scottish. This series aims to provide a view across the mosaic of that history from its earliest beginnings to the present day; each volume covers one individual aspect of the panorama but the themes are interwoven: kings and queens, heraldry and houses, wars and warriors, stained glass and churches – all link to create a tapestry of Scotland's vigorous past and her historic present.

The identity of the kings and queens of Scotland developed from Dark Age chieftains of a land scarcely larger than modern Perthshire to supreme rulers of the whole of the United Kingdom. This volume follows the story of the expansion of their domain, highlighting the fluctuating relations with the monarchs to the south. It shows how precarious was the hold on land and power, sudden death of a spouse or a child putting succession and consequently security of the realm at risk. Yet government was maintained, the edifice of state was supported, with the spiritual and political support of the Church, and monarchs survived to travel their kingdom and even, as the final section of this book describes, to enjoy some leisure. A picture emerges of just what it meant to be a monarch of the Scottish realm.

ALEXANDRA SHEPHERD
Series Editor

INTRODUCTION

Apart from highlighting one very tragic Mary, the historical spotlight seldom focuses on the lives of Scotland's kings and queens. Yet it was with the accession of a Scottish king to the English throne that the modern British state was born.

It is important to be aware of the Scottish origins of all the rulers of Britain from the early 17th century and the forces which shaped their characters. The Scottish monarchy provided a vital ingredient in the making of the United Kingdom.

The peoples of Scotland around AD 650.

The present British royal family can trace its ancestry back to the mid-9th-century rulers of a kingdom centred on present-day Perthshire. These kings could in their turn trace their ancestry further into the remote past as kings of the Gaelic speaking *Scotti* who migrated from Ulster to Argyll. This book looks back at those first kings of Picts and Scots and from them and the origins of the medieval kingdom to the Union of the crowns.

In a book of this size it is not possible to follow in detail the lives of each and every monarch; instead we look at the part they played in the evolution of the kingdom and how their rule and government was maintained and upheld. To do this the book is divided into two sections: the first three chapters explore the origins and development of the medieval kingdom, tracing its growth from the unification of the Picts and *Scots* in the 9th century down to the realisation of its rulers' long cherished ambition with the accession of James VI to the throne of England as James I in 1603. These chapters take the form of a broadly chronological narrative which charts the route by which the

The Scottish Crown: there is no more potent a symbol of monarchy and independence, but until the coronation of David II in 1331, Scotland's rulers were simply enthroned rather than crowned. The present crown is the oldest to survive in Britain, having escaped destruction in the mid-17th century to be rediscovered in the early 19th (Historic Scotland).

king of the Scots moved from being just one among several rulers in the area which we now recognise as Scotland to being one of only two fully matured monarchies in the British Isles to have survived the Middle Ages. A central theme in this narrative is the stormy relationship with England. It was a relationship with many positive aspects, one from which Scotland's rulers drew much inspiration in their state-building ventures, but it was in its spectacular collapse in the blood and bitterness of the Wars of Independence that its chief legacy lay. Born out of that struggle for survival was a powerful sense of nationhood and self-conscious awareness of a uniquely Scottish identity, strong enough to survive even the departure of its resident ruler to England in 1603.

A reconstruction of the rediscovery of the Honours of Scotland (crown, sceptre and sword of state) by Sir Walter Scott in Edinburgh Castle in 1818 (Historic Scotland).

Other threads which run through this narrative are those of the use of marriage alliances with rival states, particularly England, to build a stronger realm and the expedients demanded by the accession of kings and queens who were still merely children, subject to the manipulation of the great magnates.

In the remaining four chapters the focus shifts to examination of aspects of government and kingcraft. It is all too easy to concentrate too heavily on the individuals who wore the crown and to neglect the mechanisms through which they governed. While the offices and officers of state may lack the colour of their royal master, they are a vital component in the success story that was Scottish medieval kingship. Equally vital was the complex interrelationship of Crown and Church, a partnership which immeasurably strengthened the monarchy in its early centuries, provided a central bastion in the struggle for independence, and which provided later kings with a means of tightening control over the kingdom. But kingcraft is made of more than just the complex interplay of Church and State, and we will look too at the conscious projection of a kingly image which coloured even their leisure activities.

A 19th-century view of the Palace of Holyroodhouse, Edinburgh: the royal palace was developed in the 16th century out of the guesthouse of Holyrood Abbey. By the 1600s it had come to symbolise the continuity of an absentee, London-based monarchy, and was rebuilt by Charles II as an assertion of his authority over his Scottish realm. It remains the official residence of the reigning monarch in Scotland.

Many aspects of these kings and queens can be found in royalty everywhere but throughout they display facets unique to this land, colouring and defining the realm of Scotland which they did so much to create.

CHAPTER 1

THE NATION-BUILDERS

In the middle of the 9th century AD northern Britain experienced a long period of traumatic upheaval as first raiders then colonists from Scandinavia descended on these islands. Ancient realms, some descended from the tribes who had fought the might of Imperial Rome, were swept away in a tide of fire and blood.

The invaders carved out colonies for themselves in northern England, the Hebrides and Orkney, while the survivors of the Viking onslaught rebuilt their kingdoms from the wreckage of the old. Chief amongst these in the north was a new monarchy centred on the fertile strath of the River Earn in modern **Perthshire** and extending eastwards into **Fife** and **Angus** and northwards into **Atholl.** This

OPPOSITE: *Dumbarton Rock, Dumbartonshire: stark monument to the least well known of the kingdoms absorbed into the Scottish monarchy, this fortress-crowned rock towering above the Clyde was the citadel of the Strathclyde Britons and became an enduring symbol of royal might (Oram).*

The face of a Pict: a carving on stone from one of the early concentrations of Pictish power at Rhynie, Aberdeenshire (Shepherd).

c.785	
CONSTANTINE, KING OF PICTS	
800	
820	
OENGUS, KING OF PICTS	
834	
EOGANAN, KING OF PICTS	
Vikings destroy Pictish army	839
KENNETH I MAC ALPIN	850
DONALD I	858
CONSTANTINE I	862
AED	877
GIRIC AND EOCHAID	878
DONALD II	889
900	900
1st Battle of Corbridge	914
2nd Battle of Corbridge	918
CONSTANTINE II	
Battle of Brunanburh	937
	943
Scots gain control of Cumbria	945
MALCOLM I	950
Scots occupy Edinburgh and annexe Lothian	954
INDULF	
DUB	962
CULEN	966
OLAF	971
	977
KENNETH II	
CONSTANTINE III	995
KENNETH III	997
	1005
Battle of Carham - Scots annexe region down to Tweed	1018
MALCOLM II	
DUNCAN I	1034
	1040
MACBETH	1050
Macbeth loses control of Southern Scotland	1054
LULACH	1057
	1058
MALCOLM III	

kingdom arose from the a fusion of two Celtic peoples, the Picts, inhabitants of the north and east of what we know as Scotland, and the Scots, descended from Irish colonists, the *Scotti*, who settled in Argyll and the southern Hebrides in the 5th and 6th centuries. Their union has traditionally been represented as a simple takeover of the Pictish kingship by the Scottish ruler, Kenneth mac Alpin, but it was a far more complex process, the product of generations of warfare and gradual cultural assimilation rather than the achievement of a single event.

THE FIRST KINGS

Picts and **Scots** shared a common Celtic heritage, producing many similarities in their culture and society which were gradually strenghthened by intermarriage and the influences of the Scottish Church. It was largely through religious contacts that a *Scottish* Gaelic culture entered Pictland and began the Gaelicising of the Pictish ruling classes in the 6th and 7th centuries. Despite Scottish cultural dominance, it was the Picts who seemed set to absorb their neighbours: indeed, several 8th-century Pictish kings also ruled the Scots. Union was almost achieved in the early 9th century as a new and aggressive Pictish monarchy expanded its influence, but fate intervened: in 839 the Pictish king, **Eoghanan**, and his kingdom's chief men were slaughtered by a Viking army.

Eoghanan was not the last Pictish king, but the monarchy built by his predecessors disintegrated on his death. Several short-lived successors followed him, but the weakened Picts could not maintain overlordship of the Scots. Soon after 839, **Kenneth mac Alpin** emerged as king of the *Scottish* kingdom in Argyll. Almost immediately he marched east in a bid to re-establish a joint kingship of Picts and Scots. Details of how he achieved this are lost, but somehow, between 842 and 847, he gained mastery of the heartland of Pictish power, destroying the remnants of the Pictish dynasty in the process.

Kenneth's reign is often taken as a new departure which marked the 'creation' of the kingdom of Scotland. While the numbering of Scottish kings, for example, begins with him, and later generations looked to his time to justify claims to lordship over all territory to which the label Scotland was applied, more significantly, in his lifetime he was known as 'king of the Picts and the Scots', successor to the dual monarchy of the Pictish kings. To contemporaries, there was little sign of change. Kenneth's kingdom comprised the heart of the region over which Eoghanan had wielded power yet even as he established control over the south, a rival dynasty was embedding itself in Moray, a region where Scottish authority was weak.

The society of Kenneth's time was significantly different from that of Eoghanan's realm: Pictish language and culture had practically disappeared, replaced by the Gaelic of the new rulers. The most striking symbol of the emergence of the new monarchy, however, was a name. Old terms no longer fitted the kingdom over which Kenneth's heirs ruled. Its greater power and aspirations to wider overlordship called for something new. The name chosen was **Alba**, a Gaelic term originally applied to the whole island of Britain, but now redefined as an expression of the territory ruled by Scottish kings. With it, the medieval kingdom of Scotland was born.

MASTERS OF NORTH BRITAIN

The birth of the new kingdom coincided with the **Viking** onslaught on Britain. Norsemen from Orkney threatened the territory of the Moray kings, while the Hebrides were overwhelmed by a tide of colonists. From the south, Danes from York and Dublin struck the Scots and their neighbours, the Britons of Strathclyde. Without doubt it was an epic struggle, and the survival of Alba while older realms failed is testimony to the dynamism of Kenneth's heirs.

Kenneth's Kingdom

The Scotland of which Kenneth was the first king was not the Scotland of today. The heartland of his power lay in Tayside, although he may well have extended his authority north over the lands around the Moray Firth. As late as 900 the effective boundaries of his descendants' kingdom lay on the Spey in the north, the Forth in the south and the mountains of Drumalban in the west.

SHETLAND

ORKNEY

SCANDINAVIAN LANDS

MORAY

KINGDOM OF THE PICTS AND SCOTS

St Andrews

Forteviot

Dunkeld

Dunadd

Dunbarton

STRATHCLYDE

NORTHUMBRIA

Scotland c. AD 850.

Bamburgh, Northumberland: ancient citadel of the Bernician kings, long coveted by the Scots. Failure to capture this strategic fortress which dominates the Northumberland plain baulked Scottish ambitions to occupy the lands between the Tweed and the Tees in England (Oram).

Sueno's Stone, Forres, Moray: it was in battles, such as those commemorated on this monumental sculpture, that the Scottish kingdom was born. Rather than the sterile account of victory and defeat recorded in the pages of early chronicles, here we can see the full horror of war, the celebration of victory, and the bloody consequences of defeat (Oram).

By 900, survival turned to expansion. Under **Constantine II**, grandson of Kenneth mac Alpin, the Scots emerged as a major power. His ambitions lay in the south, where control of Strathclyde opened the road to **Bernicia**, a land sandwiched between the Scots and Scandinavian York. Having made Bernicia a Scottish dependency, Constantine sought to draw York into his orbit: he failed. Instead, York fell under English domination. Constantine, however, preferred a weak York on his southern border to a powerful English kingdom. In 937 he allied himself with the Scandinavian king of Dublin, claimant to the throne of York, and assembled an army to challenge the English king, Athelstan, for mastery of Britain.

The decisive conflict came at Brunanburh, deep in English territory. There, Athelstan defeated the Scots, the Strathclyde Britons, and the Scandinavians of York and Dublin, confirming his grip on York. On his death, however, in 939, the king of Dublin seized the city back but had to turn to Constantine for protection in the face of renewed English hostility. Thus, when Constantine resigned the kingship in 943 to become a monk, he left a kingdom whose influence extended to the Humber.

This domination was short-lived, however, and York passed back into English hands in 952. Meanwhile, Constantine and his successor, **Malcolm I**, had secured lordship over **Strathclyde** and **Lothian**. Full control of Lothian was gained by Constantine's son, **Indulf**, who reigned from 954 to 962. He capitalised on temporary English weakness to seize Edinburgh and annexe Lothian. But the Scots also sought lordship in the north, where they faced an aggressive rival in Scandinavian Orkney, which brought Caithness and Sutherland under its domination by 900. Constantine II used alliances with these Viking earls to force Moray into submission, but the southward spread of Orkney power was as much a threat to Constantine's successors as it was to the Northerners. Towards the end of his reign, Indulf faced a Scandinavian challenge for mastery of the Moray Firth region, and it was at Cullen in 962 that he fell in battle with a Viking army.

SUCCESS OF AN AGGRESSIVE LINE

Indulf's death was followed by a protracted and bloody struggle for the kingship. In such circumstances, little progress was made in the expansion of the kingdom, until in 1005 **Malcolm II** mac Kenneth eliminated his rivals and established his line's monopoly on the succession. Free from challenge at home, Malcolm resumed the southward drive. In 1018, at Carham on the Tweed, he crushed the Bernicians and won control of Lothian down to the Tweed. Victory brought bonuses: amongst casualties on the Scottish side was Owain, king of Strathclyde, last of a family who ruled as vassals of the Scots. Following Owain's death, Malcolm occupied Strathclyde.

Amongst the factors which permitted Malcolm to push south was increased influence in Orkney. This coincided with a feud in the **Moray** dynasty which Malcolm let fester – it kept Moray weak – but

Dunsinnan Hill, Perthshire: tradition records this as the scene of Malcolm Canmore's decisive victory over Macbeth in 1054. It is possible that Macbeth had reoccupied the ancient fortress which crowns this strategic hilltop overlooking the fertile Vale of Strathmore (Oram).

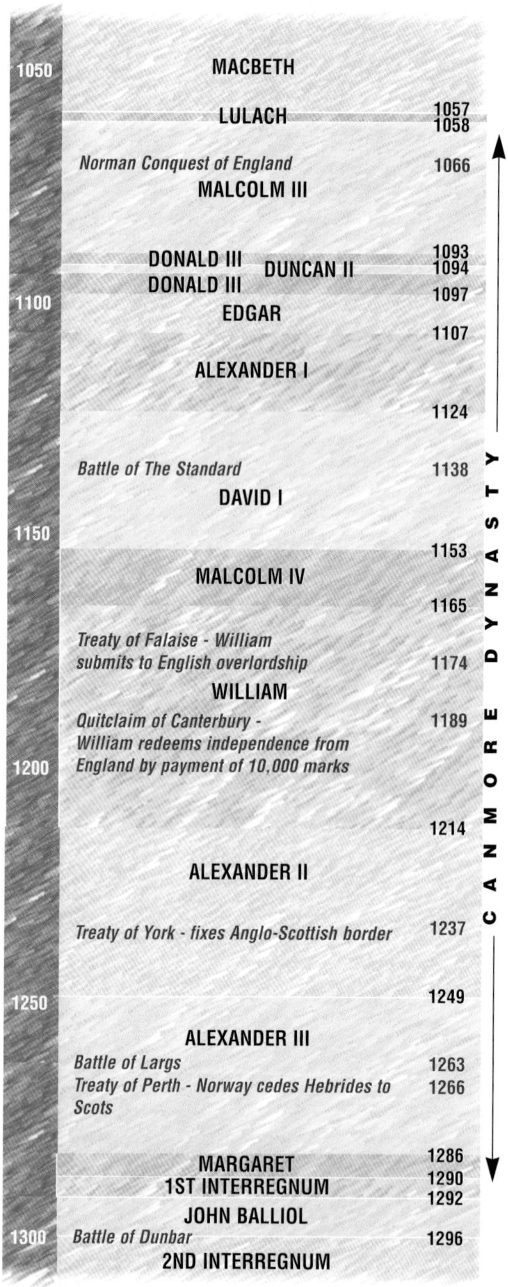
1050
MACBETH
LULACH 1057 1058
Norman Conquest of England 1066
MALCOLM III
DONALD III 1093
DUNCAN II 1094
DONALD III 1097
1100
EDGAR
1107
ALEXANDER I
1124
Battle of The Standard 1138
DAVID I
1150
1153
MALCOLM IV
1165
Treaty of Falaise - William submits to English overlordship 1174
WILLIAM
Quitclaim of Canterbury - William redeems independence from England by payment of 10,000 marks 1189
1200
1214
ALEXANDER II
Treaty of York - fixes Anglo-Scottish border 1237
1249
1250
ALEXANDER III
Battle of Largs 1263
Treaty of Perth - Norway cedes Hebrides to Scots 1266
MARGARET 1286
1ST INTERREGNUM 1290
JOHN BALLIOL 1292
1300
Battle of Dunbar 1296
2ND INTERREGNUM
CANMORE DYNASTY

this had dangerous implications. The feud climaxed in 1020 with the murder of Findlaech of Moray by his nephews, who ruled in succession down to 1032, when Macbeth, Findlaech's son, with Malcolm II's encouragement, avenged his father by burning his cousin to death in his hall.

Malcolm's enthusiastic elimination of rivals ensured the smooth accession of his grandson, **Duncan I**. Duncan inherited Malcolm's ambition but lacked his ability. The image of invulnerability created by Malcolm was undermined by defeats, culminating in a rout at Durham in 1039. Discontent grew, and Macbeth, who at first served Duncan loyally, became the focus for opposition, especially after his marriage to Gruoch, a descendent of a rival line which Malcolm had sought to destroy. In an attempt to nip the threat from Moray in the bud, in 1040 Duncan marched north. The result was catastrophe, with the king dying at the hands of Macbeth's warriors. Seizing the initiative, **Macbeth** raced south and, although he failed to capture or kill Duncan's sons, took hold of the throne.

'ALL HAIL, MACBETH! THAT SHALT BE KING HEREAFTER!'

Powerful forces remained loyal to Duncan's heirs, and unwelcome interest was attracted by the drama of Macbeth's accession: both Thorfinn, earl of Orkney, and Siward, earl of Northumbria, saw opportunities for gain. In 1045, Duncan's father, Crinan, rebelled in the name of his grandson, Malcolm. His rebellion drew support from Siward, who occupied Lothian, but Crinan himself was defeated and killed by Macbeth. In the north, Thorfinn, himself a grandson of Malcolm II, achieved a string of victories over Macbeth, but failed to topple him from power.

Macbeth's weakness lay in his failure to eliminate Duncan's sons. In 1054 the eldest, Malcolm, aided by Siward, defeated Macbeth in a battle. It was a costly victory, for Siward's eldest son, Osbeorn, was killed, and it failed in its objective: Macbeth escaped. Siward, nevertheless, controlled Scotland south of the Mounth, and there he set up Duncan's son, Malcolm Canmore, as **Malcolm III**. Fortunately for the Scots, however, Siward died in 1055 and his successor could not maintain lordship over southern Scotland.

In 1057, Malcolm III carried the war into Moray. Macbeth intercepted Malcolm's army in southern Aberdeenshire, but was overwhelmed and slain. His death did not bring the collapse of his cause, for the men of Moray proclaimed his stepson, **Lulach**, king of Scots. Seven months later, in March 1058, Malcolm slew Lulach and marched into Moray.

THE CANMORE DREAM

The shape of Scotland c. AD 1000–1050.

Malcolm's victory in 1058 saw him gain unprecedented control over the north. The key to this lay in an understanding with his kinsman, Thorfinn, Earl of Orkney, whose daughter, Ingibjorg, Malcolm married. The product of this marriage was a level of stability not seen in the region since the 9th century, which permitted Malcolm to focus attention on other matters.

Malcolm cherished ambitions to extend his domain southwards. Despite becoming 'sworn brother' of Tostig, Earl of Northumbria, Malcolm used the earl's absence on pilgrimage to raid his earldom. It brought plunder, but no increase in territory. Nevertheless, it set the pattern for the future. A golden opportunity came in 1065 when Tostig was expelled by his brother, King Harold of England, and fled to Scotland. Malcolm planned to aid Tostig to recover his lands and put him in his debt, but Tostig preferred an alliance with the Norwegians, which ended in his death in battle near York. This lost chance opened a fresh opportunity for Scottish gain, for while **Harold** had been dealing with his brother, **William of Normandy** landed on the

19

A lost opportunity? The Norman invasion of England in 1066 and their destruction of the Anglo-Saxon king, Harold II, and his army at Hastings caught the Scots unprepared for this unlooked-for chance to seize control of Northumbria. Depiction of the death of Harold from a facsimile of the Bayeux Tapestry.

English south coast. Harold's death and the decimation of the Anglo-Saxon leadership at Hastings created a power vacuum in northern England which Malcolm sought to fill.

The flight to Scotland in 1068 of **Edgar**, claimant to the English throne, with his mother, and sisters, opened new avenues. In 1069–70, Edgar and his friends invaded England in a bid for the throne, but Malcolm held back. The invasion failed and in 1070 Edgar and his family returned to Scotland. Only then did Malcolm act, harrying all the way to the Tees in an effort to subdue a province already wasted by William's armies. It was a brutal campaign and did nothing to win over people who might have preferred his dominion to that of the Normans. Once again he had failed to achieve anything.

Malcolm tried new tactics. By 1069 he was a widower, and marriage to one of Edgar's sisters was politically attractive. This was a threatening development for William, who feared Malcolm's intervention in England. In 1072 he launched a pre-emptive invasion of Scotland, the greatest incursion since 934. It was not aimed at conquest, its objective being to bring Malcolm to heel. He submitted and agreed to expel Edgar and his supporters, hand over important hostages and give William homage.

Malcolm stood by his word until 1079. Again he miscalculated, but again he escaped with lenient terms, which encouraged him to view this submission as no more meaningful than previous treaties. This readiness to break pacts, even when reinforced by oaths, sits uneasily with his pious reputation fabricated by later generations. The last three years of his reign show how little Malcolm valued his pledges. Opportunist to the end, in 1091 he used William II's absence from England to ravage Northumbria. Faced by William's army, Malcolm submitted, in return receiving promises of the restoration of lands in England. By 1093 it was clear that the Norman king was not fulfilling his side of the treaty. Dissatisfied with the terms offered, Malcolm raised an army which crossed the border in early November. On 13 November his dream of expansion ended in bloody rout at **Alnwick**, leaving the king and Edward, his eldest son by Margaret, dead on the field.

CELTIC TWILIGHT

The deaths of Malcolm and his heir threw the kingdom into confusion. Amidst much uncertainty, the nobles turned to the senior male in the royal kindred, Malcolm's brother, **Donald Ban**. Often portrayed as a traditionalist struggling against the tide of history, he was the front-man for a powerful group of nobles who resented foreign influence and effected a backlash against English cultural influence at court. Instead of the xenophobic reaction of a Celtic die-hard, the expulsion of the clique which had surrounded his brother was a calculated blow against the likely focus of opposition to his succession, Malcolm's remaining sons by Margaret.

Malcolm's exiled family pinned its hopes on English support. William II saw the potential in this dependence and in 1094 named Malcolm's surviving son by Ingibjorg, **Duncan II**, as vassal-king of Scotland. Duncan depended on the knights whom William sent to aid him, and after these withdrew he was killed in a revolt. William did not give up, and in 1095 invested Malcolm's eldest surviving son by Margaret, **Edgar**, as his vassal. It was only in 1097, however, that Edgar overcame his rivals.

Edgar remained loyal to William, and his reign is remarkable only for an indifference towards his Celtic heritage and disinterest in Church affairs. Lack of interest in his Celtic past was revealed in 1098 in a treaty which recognised Norse rule in the Hebrides. Amongst the islands abandoned was **Iona**, spiritual heart of Celtic Scotland and burial place of Scottish kings since 858. The reign of Edgar's successor, his younger brother **Alexander I**, marked a new departure. In contrast to Edgar, Alexander was based in the Scottish heartland, but he too was a vassal of the English king. His dependence was confirmed in 1114 when he participated in an English campaign in Wales.

Malcolm's Saintly Queen. Remembered chiefly for her religious works, Margaret's canonisation in 1250 cast the lustre of a saintly ancestor on the royal dynasty. This modern stained-glass depiction is from St Margaret's Chapel, Edinburgh Castle (Historic Scotland).

Duffus Castle, Moray. Victory over the ruler of Moray in 1130 saw David begin the century-long process of colonisation of northern Scotland. Plantation of foreign colonists based on powerful new fortresses, such as that at Duffus built by Freskin the Fleming, underpinned Scottish control of the territories (Shepherd).

Innovations of David I

David introduced foreign clerics to undertake the reform of the Church. Towns, too, formed a central element in his reconstruction programme. Town-like communities existed in Scotland before 1124, but David began urban development with crown support. He granted charters of privileges, guaranteeing legal rights and local trade monopolies, and established such communities as royal burghs. The burghs were channels for trade with the Continent, and marked the expansion of royal power into the economic life of the land. Image of David I from a silver penny (Shepherd).

THE REVOLUTIONARY KING

In 1124, the childless Alexander I was succeeded by his remaining brother, **David I**. David had made his career at the court of **Henry I** of England, and a future as an English nobleman seemed assured when in 1114 Henry gave him Maud de Senlis, Countess of Northampton, as his wife. She brought David the resources to develop his Scottish lands, and he began to introduce English administrative practices as tools to strengthen his grip. Knights from his English lands served as warrior-administrators, while a French cleric appointed bishop of Glasgow oversaw the reform of the Church. With Lothian and Strathclyde secure, and a body of foreign knights and clergymen behind him, he had a well-established base from which to construct a dynamic new style of kingship for Scotland. Although he enjoyed good relations with the Celtic nobles north of the Forth, it was in Lothian that he consolidated his power and it was there that the most significant changes were wrought during his reign.

His years saw an influx of aristocratic colonists who received land throughout southern Scotland. These incomers brought dependants, and where they settled rapid anglicisation of local society and culture occurred.

Alongside innovations of Church reform and town development, David made shifts in policy with far-reaching consequences

22

for his kingdom. The first was in **Moray**, which was invaded in 1130 and subdued by garrisons based on a string of castles which controlled the route from Aberdeen to Inverness: final conquest of the north had begun. David's attention, however, was diverted to England. In 1135, Henry I died, leaving his daughter, **Matilda**, David's niece, as heir. David, with the English barons, had sworn to accept her succession, but instead Henry's nephew, **Stephen**, husband of another of David's nieces, seized the throne. In 1136, as opposition to Stephen mounted, David made his play. His support for Matilda was tempered by personal concerns: through reviving hereditary title and military pressure, David occupied Cumberland and Northumberland. Despite defeat at the Battle of the Standard in 1138, David integrated both areas into his kingdom and in 1149 came within an ace of adding York to his domain. At his death in 1153, David had transformed the kingdom and left the monarchy immeasurably stronger. No previous Scottish king had enjoyed such power, and he appeared to have decisively altered the balance of power in north Britain.

The Scotland of David I c. AD 1150.

MALCOLM IV

The new king, David's grandson **Malcolm IV**, was a boy of 12. He immediately faced rebellion as areas kept quiescent under David sought to throw off Scottish lordship. Risings in Ross and Argyll, which erupted within months of David's death, rumbled on into the 1160s, overlapping with disturbances in Moray and Galloway, but none threatened to unseat Malcolm. Instead, royal power continued its advance into unstable zones, such as Clydesdale where Malcolm planted a colony of Flemings, or Kyle and Renfrew where he built up the power of the Stewart dynasty. Such policies provoked further hostile reaction from the Celtic lords, but risings were ruthlessly and efficiently suppressed.

Malcolm's difficulties increased in 1154, when **Henry II** ascended the English throne. Henry aimed to regain northern England and, using promises and threats, secured its return in 1157. Unease grew

Although he bore a Celtic name, Malcolm IV showed little affinity with his Celtic subjects, trusting instead the foreign incomers in his household, and embracing the chivalric ideals of Anglo–French culture.

New powers in the land. The Stewart family marked its entry into the upper ranks of the nobility in the 1160s by foundation of Paisley Abbey in the heart of their lordship of Renfrew. Their establishment as royal agents in the Clyde estuary region tightened crown control in an area where its power was previously weak. They defeated Somerled, semi-independent ruler of Argyll, and, stepping into the vacuum created by his death, swiftly gained control of Bute and Cowal (Oram).

in 1159 when Malcolm and his brother, William, accompanied Henry on a campaign to Toulouse: such service smacked of vassaldom. Furthermore, the jaunt suggested indifference towards royal responsibilities. The result was an unsuccessful attempt to curb foreign influence at court and awaken the king to his duties. Its failure demonstrated the increase in royal power since the 1120s, and revealed the dominance of the foreign families introduced by David. With the support of those knights, Malcolm overcame the rebels and pressed on with David's innovative policies.

THE CHAINED LION

Malcolm's death in 1165 brought his brother, **William**, to the throne. His reign was the longest in medieval Scotland, but its length is no measure of success. On the contrary, William led Scotland further into English overlordship, and ended his reign dependent on English aid to maintain his authority. His personal failures, however, should not distract from the positive achievements of his reign, which saw continuing expansion of royal power into the peripheries of the realm and development of the machinery of government.

William was obsessed with recovering northern England, and in 1173 used a rebellion against Henry to further this ambition. Disaster followed: in July 1174 he was captured and forced into the Treaty of Falaise, which involved submission to Henry and recognition of his overlordship. Defeat triggered risings in Galloway, lasting until 1186, and in Ross where Donald Macwilliam, a direct descendant of Duncan II, threatened to overturn Scottish gains. In 1179, William campaigned in person in Moray, but only in 1187 was Macwilliam finally defeated and killed.

William faced constant reminders of English domination: his fortresses held English garrisons; he was required to seek Henry's council and explain his actions in Scotland. A further reminder of overlordship came when Henry arranged William's marriage. But the clipping of William's wings did bring positive results for he threw

In 1208 the English King John's strengthening of his castle at Norham on the River Tweed, and building of a fort at Tweedmouth, brought Scotland and England to the brink of war. King William backed away from conflict and in August 1209 at Norham he submitted to John (Oram).

himself into the government of Scotland with energy. From this stemmed his reputation as an upholder of the law, earning the later epithet of 'lion of justice'.

Subjection ended when **Richard I** of England, seeking to finance his Crusade, sold his overlordship in 1189 for 10,000 merks. Following his success in Ross and Galloway, this brought William to the height of his powers and the 1190s witnessed a return to

What price freedom? To secure his release from English captivity, William agreed to the humiliating terms of the Treaty of Falaise. In addition to recognition of Henry II's overlordship, William was required to surrender five key fortresses, including his great castle at Edinburgh, into the hands of English garrisons whose upkeep was paid by the Scots (Historic Scotland).

aggressive expansion. Campaigns into the far north in 1196–1197 saw the submission of Caithness, while royal supervision over Galloway was tightened. By 1200, William held unprecedented authority over an enlarged sphere of royal power.

The last decade of William's reign saw decline. Old age and ill health plagued the king and, with his son, Alexander, still a child, Scotland suffered from lack of leadership. The English king, **John**, exploited this situation: in 1209 he extorted the right to arrange the marriages of William's daughters. On the heels of this came rebellion in Ross. The ailing king responded with unexpected energy, but in 1212 he turned to John for aid. Assistance came at a price: the right to arrange the marriage of William's heir. Overlordship may not have been explicitly conceded, but William's legacy to Alexander was English domination restored to pre-1189 levels.

DAWN OF THE GOLDEN AGE

The reign of **Alexander II** (1214–1249) saw the kingdom reach maturity, and the Canmores achieve total control of mainland Scotland. Alexander benefited from the wealth which the reorganised royal administration and expanding trade brought, but this should not

Master of mainland Scotland

Co-operation with Church and nobility underlay Alexander II's success. His domestic power strengthened dealings with England: there was no question of submission to overlordship. In 1238, the widowed, childless Alexander demonstrated his independence by marrying Marie de Coucy, a relative of the French king. Scotland was taking its place on the international stage. The Great Seal of Alexander II shows the king as an armoured knight on his horseback.

obscure his personal contribution to state formation. From the outset, Alexander aimed to recover full independence. Rebellion in England opened the way, and in 1215 Alexander allied with John's enemies and laid claim to northern England: by 1216 he controlled Carlisle. The defeat of the rebels by supporters of John's son, **Henry III**, left Alexander dangerously exposed and in 1217 he made peace and yielded up his conquests, but the English were in no position to reimpose overlordship. New solutions had to be found for the dispute over the frontier between the kingdoms: a move towards stability came in 1221 when Alexander married Henry's sister, Joan. Only in 1237, however, was the issue resolved by the Treaty of York, wherein Alexander renounced his ancestral claims.

Peace with England let Alexander concentrate on domestic issues. A northern rising in 1214 was crushed with the support of a Celtic

Scotland in AD 1249.

lord from Ross, who understood the rewards of co-operation. To consolidate this new hold, however, he had to settle the issue of control of Argyll and the Isles, for those areas – and Ireland – provided his Macwilliam enemies with both mercenary troops and a back door into Scotland.

The 1220s saw westwards expansion in which royal power was carried to the frontiers of **Argyll**. Domination of the Clyde estuary saw the building of Tarbert Castle as a springboard into the Hebrides. Alexander also encouraged Alan of Galloway's private war with the Manx, for domination of Man would close another conduit of aid for the Macwilliams. This backfired: Alan destabilised a volatile region and prompted Manx appeals for aid from Norway. It was a major crisis, full-scale war being averted only with difficulty. For the Macwilliams, however, defeat resulted in elimination.

Now at the height of his power, Alexander embarked on the reconquest of the **Isles**. Continued instability in the Hebrides threatened Alexander's control of the West Highlands. The ambiguous relationships of Hebridean lords, such as the MacDougalls of Lorn who held Argyll from the King of Scots and adjacent islands like Mull from the Norwegian Crown, needed clarification. Negotiations came to nothing, so Alexander opted for confrontation. When MacDougall failed to give acceptable assurances, Alexander mounted a massive campaign by land and sea. On 8 July 1249, as his fleet lay off the island of Kerrera in Oban Bay, poised to complete the four-century long process of building the kingdom, Alexander II died.

Dunstaffnage. In 1249 Alexander II was poised to complete his grip on Argyll and the Isles with a campaign to force the MacDougall lords of Lorn into submission – his target, Dunstaffnage, chief stronghold of the MacDougalls. Poised to strike, Alexander died on the island of Kerrera and his host melted away (Oram).

MEDIEVAL HIGH NOON

The king's death heralded a further period of instability, as his son, **Alexander III**, was eight. Rival factions seeking control of government turned to England for aid. Henry III's influence in Scottish affairs was strengthened in 1251 when Alexander married Henry's daughter. Throughout the minority, however, the issue of overlordship remained dormant, and Alexander's assumption of full power in 1258–59 removed any opportunity for English intervention. The family relationship between Alexander and Henry saw the issue fall into the background, while political crisis in England meant that Henry was in no position to press his claims.

Henry's difficulties permitted Alexander to complete the conquest of the Isles. Negotiations for a peaceful transfer failed, and Scottish raids prompted a Norwegian response: in 1263 the Norwegian fleet arrived in Orkney, but only in mid-August did it enter the Hebrides, reaching the Clyde in September. There was no showdown. Instead gales stranded Norwegian ships at Largs and their crews skirmished with local levies in a brawl since dignified with the title **Battle of Largs**. Recognising that time was against him, the Norwegian king withdrew to Orkney to overwinter, where, after a short illness, he died.

Alexander III, from the depiction of his inauguration in a 15th-century manuscript of Fordun's Scotichronicon (Shepherd).

This marked the end of Norwegian control of the Isles. In spring 1264 negotiations resumed, while the Scots raided the Hebrides and took the submission of local chieftains. By the time formal transfer of overlordship to the Scots was agreed in the Treaty of Perth, Man and the Isles had already accepted Alexander's lordship. Scotland had reached its medieval apogee, with only Orkney and Shetland to add to its territory in future. Alexander had achieved his ancestors' ambition: he was now not simply king of Scots, but the only king in Scotland.

29

CHAPTER 2

THE FIGHT FOR INDEPENDENCE

T he processes of unification and expansion which we traced in Chapter 1 led to the formation of a kingdom with a strong sense of identity and cohesion. Within barely three decades of the gaining of the Isles, however, that unity and cohesion was to be tested to the full in a life and death struggle with the only other developed kingdom within the British Isles: England.

OPPOSITE: *Although his place in popular tradition has now been somewhat usurped by William Wallace, Robert Bruce carved his place in history as the man who regained Scotland's independence. This tableau of his coronation is from Edinburgh Castle (Historic Scotland).*

From the 10th century, the status of the kings of Scotland towards the kings of England was a recurring source of antagonism. Submissions, such as those made by Constantine II to Athelstan, had signalled recognition of English military superiority. By the 11th century, however, interpretation of submissions was changing, with emphasis being placed on the bonds forged within the process. Instead of marking acceptance of temporary domination by the greater power of a neighbouring king, acts of submission became recognitions of subservience which bestowed rights on the overlord to the service of his vassal. This change underlay the repeated submissions of Malcolm III to the Norman kings: Malcolm viewed them as temporary expedients, the Normans saw them as binding agreements. To English kings, such submissions were regarded as absolute recognition of their lordship over Scotland.

Overlordship was not an issue while Scotland and England remained on friendly terms. David I's family ties with Henry I of England rendered rigid bonds unnecessary, and when

Tradition records that the Saltire, or St Andrew's Cross, appeared in the heavens as an omen of victory for the Scots over their Anglo-Saxon enemies. By the 14th century it had been adopted as a national talisman in the independence struggle (Shepherd).

MARGARET 1ST INTERREGNUM	1290 1292	
JOHN BALLIOL		
Battle of Dunbar	1296	
2ND INTERREGNUM		
	1306	
Death of Edward I of England	1309	
Battle of Bannockburn	1314	
ROBERT I		
	1329	
Battle of Halidon Hill	1333	
Battle of Neville's Cross	1346	
DAVID II		
Treaty of Berwick - Ransoming of David II	1357	
Accession of Stewarts	1371	
ROBERT II		

(Vertical label alongside timeline: BRUCE DYNASTY)

that relationship broke down in the 1130s, the English crown was in no position to assert its claims. The misadventures of the Scottish kings after 1153 opened the door to domination, but Henry II was content to have his rights recognised rather than pressed. In the 13th century, however, Henry's successors, having lost their continental empire, sought to extend within Britain and redefine relationships with varying degrees of success, capitalising on periodic Scottish weakness.

GATHERING CLOUDS

Alexander III's reign was a time of peace and prosperity. His objectives had changed: consolidation of power, integration of acquisitions, and maintenance of the partnership between king and nobility, became priorities. His task was aided by economic growth: prosperity benefited royal coffers and produced a 'feel good factor' among the populace. Scottish stability gave weight to Alexander's stature. Self-confident of his own status, there was no question of accepting English overlordship: the family relationship between the rulers of both kingdoms saw the issue remain in abeyance, although

Alexander III's successful reign ended in tragedy below this monument at Pettycur, in Fife. Having left Edinburgh and crossed the Forth in the teeth of a gale, he was thrown from his horse and killed as he galloped along the rocky shore towards Kinghorn (Oram).

occasional airing kept its future revival possible. In 1274, when Alexander travelled to London to attend the coronation of his brother-in-law, Edward I, his presence was in no way interpreted as an act of submission.

Close ties with England survived the death of Queen Margaret in 1275. With three living children, Alexander did not immediately re-marry. His family offered a means of increasing his European standing, for their marriages could forge ties with other powers. In 1281 his daughter, Margaret, married King Eric of

Norway, while in 1282 his elder son, Alexander, married Margaret, daughter of the Count of Flanders, strengthening links with one of Scotland's major trading partners. High hopes were placed in both marriages, but Margaret died in 1283, after giving birth to a daughter, also named Margaret, while in 1284 Alexander died childless. As his younger brother, David, had died in 1281, the Canmore succession hung by the slender thread of a sickly child in Norway.

Faced with the uncertainty of a female succession, Alexander re-married in the expectation of fathering another son. In November 1285, following his father's example of looking to France for a second bride, he married Yolande, daughter of the Count of Dreux. Five months later, Alexander, eager to return to his wife at Kinghorn in Fife, braved the storm-tossed waters of the Forth, and ignoring the advice of his companions galloped into the darkness and mounting storm. On 30 March 1286 his body was found on the foreshore near Pettycur: he had broken his neck in a fall from his horse.

THE MAID OF NORWAY

By midsummer it was clear that Yolande was not pregnant, and on 2 July **Margaret**, Maid of Norway, Alexander's grand-daughter, was proclaimed queen. With the experience of the minority of 1249–1258 behind them, the Scots set up a broad-based government to rule in Margaret's absence. Contrary to expectations, the kingdom did not fall apart in factional strife, and the achievement of the Canmore kings in forging a united land out of a patchwork of rival powers was revealed for all to see.

The accession of a queen was without precedent in Scotland. The matter of her marriage posed grave problems, for her husband would

The Orkney Islands: this was the nearest that Scotland's child-queen, Margaret of Norway, came to her kingdom. A sickly child, the stormy crossing of the North Sea broke her health, and she was carried ashore in Orkney to die, still on Norwegian territory (Shepherd).

Edward I: The myth of Edward the Judge

With so many Competitors, how were their rights to be adjudged? The Scots turned to Edward for arbitration, as he enjoyed an international reputation as a lawyer. This held dangers: having seen plans for peaceful union dashed once, Edward was unlikely to let a second opportunity slip. In 1291, as a precursor to the debate, Edward demanded recognition of his overlordship. Having received the homage and fealty of the Competitors, he outmanoeuvred the Scots and received acknowledgement of his position. Image of a young Edward from a carving at Winchester Cathedral (Shepherd).

exercise rule in her name. To avoid the tensions which marriage to a Scottish noble would produce, a foreign marriage was proposed. The obvious candidate, in view of the friendship between Alexander III and **Edward I**, was Edward's son, Edward, Prince of Wales. This had attractions: England was Scotland's principal trading partner; nobles in both kingdoms held estates on both sides of the border; and Edward had the authority to maintain stability in Scotland during the minority. It was an appealing prospect for Edward, boosting immeasurably the power of the English Crown, resolving the issue of overlordship, and removing fears of Scottish alliances with France. In July 1290, by the Treaty of Birgham, a marriage settlement which guaranteed Scottish independence was settled. Both kingdoms looked to the future with confidence in September 1290 as Margaret sailed from Norway to enter her inheritance. In early October disturbing rumours spread south from Orkney: the Maid was dead.

THE GREAT CAUSE OF SCOTLAND

Margaret's death was greeted by stunned disbelief amongst all concerned. For the Scots, the certainty of peace and continuity had been removed. For Edward, it shattered dreams of peaceful union. Despite a sense of crisis the Scots displayed remarkable political unity. But this was a kingdom without a ruler or even a recognised heir: in whose name was any government to govern? The chief problem, however, was not that there was no heir, but that there were too many claims on the throne: by the end of 1290, thirteen men had come forward as claimants.

To choose from amongst them, a court, selected by the two front-runners in the dispute – John **Balliol**, lord of Galloway, and Robert **Bruce**, lord of Annandale – plus twenty-four of Edward's nominees, was appointed to hear the disputations. Both men were descended from David, Earl of Huntingdon, brother of William the Lion, through his daughters Margaret and Isabel. John was grandson of Margaret, while Robert was son of Isabel. Although John's line was senior, it descended twice through heiresses – his mother was Margaret's elder daughter – while Robert's passed only once through the female line. The dispute, therefore, focused on precedence: John claimed seniority, but Robert was nearest in degree to the common ancestor. It may seem clear-cut in modern eyes, but in the late 13th century it revealed ambiguity in laws governing inheritance. As a result, it was not until November 1292 that a decision was reached. On 17 November, the court pronounced in favour of Balliol.

THE REIGN OF KING JOHN

John's reign (1292–1296) marked the nadir of Scottish kingship. From the outset, Edward had established his overlordship and, unlike Henry II, pressed what he regarded as his rights. This included hearing appeals from Scottish courts, and John faced the unprecedented humiliation of being summoned to explain judgements. Attempts to defy Edward met with threats of punitive action, and by September 1293 John had submitted.

For the Scots, Edward's actions were unacceptable. When he summoned John to perform military service in France in June 1294, opposition gelled into resistance. The Scots won papal absolution from oaths taken under duress, a move towards freeing themselves from promises extorted by Edward. John, however, was compromised by his submissions and, in July 1295, a council was appointed to oversee his government. In October 1295, in a bid to safeguard their independence, the Scots allied with Edward's French enemies, a provocative act: the two countries slid into war.

Hostilities opened in March 1296 when the Scots ravaged Cumberland. In response, Edward attacked Berwick, and sacked the town, butchering its people. Four weeks later, at Dunbar, he routed the Scottish army. Resistance collapsed, but Edward was in no mood for compromise. In July he presided over John's final humiliation, stripped him of his royal insignia and consigned him to the Tower of London. Determined to ensure that his overlordship was never again challenged, in August 1296 he recorded the submission of 2,000 leading Scots in the document known as Ragman Rolls. Confident of total victory, he entrusted Scottish government to the Earl of Surrey and headed for home.

The verdict of history has been harsh on John Balliol. Shown on his great seal as the successor to the majesty of his royal ancestors, John was humiliated repeatedly by his English overlord. Driven into war in 1296, he was forced into surrender and ritually stripped of the symbols of his royal office. The royal arms were ripped from his surcoat, leaving him literally 'Toom Tabard', or 'empty coat' (Shepherd).

THE KINGLESS KINGDOM

While Edward considered John deposed and his kingdom annexed to England, many Scots still regarded him as king. Others saw service to Edward as a path to power, the Bruces in particular seeking succession to the vacant throne. Spurned by Edward, however, they began a dangerous game in which family ambitions took precedence over national loyalties.

Edward's hold over Scotland proved illusory: in summer 1297 **William Wallace** and Andrew Murray, fighting in Balliol's name,

defeated Surrey at Stirling Bridge and all but drove out the English. Although Edward crushed Wallace's army at Falkirk in July 1298, he was unable to re-establish the grip enjoyed after Dunbar. Falkirk, however, ended Wallace's authority, and before the end of 1298 he was replaced as Guardian by **John Comyn** of Badenoch, and **Robert Bruce**, Earl of Carrick, grandson of the Competitor. This arrangement was doomed to failure: Robert's ambitions were incompatible with defence of the interests of the exiled king. Consequently, Robert made repeated changes of allegiance, always switching to whatever side offered the best chance of realising his royal pretensions.

In 1301 it looked as though Balliol might be restored with French aid, but in 1302 the French suffered a crushing defeat and the Scots were mere onlookers as England and France settled a peace treaty: in February 1304 they surrendered. Once again conquest seemed absolute, and Edward began to reconstruct Scotland's laws and government. In September 1305 his parliament set out a blueprint for the future which saw Scotland reduced to a mere province of the English Crown. Within months, however, it was a dead letter, swept aside as **Robert Bruce** made a final bid for the throne.

A towering figure in the pantheon of Scottish national heroes, William Wallace (statue, 1888, by W Grant Stevenson, Aberdeen) enjoys a reputation as a selfless leader of a popular revolt against English overlordship. Although most of his career is shrouded in obscurity, the myth of Wallace, the martyr for the nationalist cause, has gained worldwide acceptance (Shepherd).

The seige of Caerlaverock. In spite of his rout of Wallace's army at Falkirk in July 1298, Edward I was unable to reassert the level of control over Scotland which he enjoyed in 1296: in 1300, a major expedition into Galloway succeeded only in capturing Scottish-held Caerlaverock, the fortress which commanded the estuary of the River Nith (Historic Scotland).

USURPER OR HERO KING?

Robert had been preparing for some time, but in February 1306 he was still unready. He knew that he would have to win over the Comyns, but this would require them to abandon Balliol. A meeting with John Comyn at Greyfriars Kirk in Dumfries ended in bloodshed, with Comyn falling to Robert's dagger. Realising that he must act quickly, Robert hurried to Scone for enthronement as king. Despite Church support – it feared for its own freedom should Edward absorb Scotland into his kingdom – Robert was dangerously exposed. Not only was he a murderous usurper in the eyes of both Comyn's kin and of those loyal to Balliol, but his sacrilege meant excommunication. By late summer he was a fugitive, his army scattered, and most of his family dead or imprisoned. Furthermore, he had plunged Scotland into civil war and driven the Comyns into the welcoming arms of Edward.

Recovery appeared impossible, but there was no going back. In 1307 he began a guerilla campaign. Several small victories encouraged men to join Robert's standard, but it was the death of Edward in July 1307 that swung the pendulum decisively in Robert's favour. Deprived of the driving will of the old king – Edward II lacked the determination to prosecute the war – the English offensive withered. It was the breathing space Robert required, and by the end of 1308 he had routed the Comyns and established a firm hold over the country beyond the Forth.

Before recapturing all Scottish towns and castles still in English hands, in August 1312 Robert carried the war into England. By the summer of 1314 only Stirling of fortresses of note remained in enemy possession, and its governor agreed to surrender unless an army came to his relief before midsummer. It was a challenge which Edward II could not ignore, and the largest army to march against Scotland since 1298 was mustered for the ill-fated **Bannockburn** campaign.

Bannockburn

Victory at Bannockburn set the seal on Robert's success. The English, ill-disciplined and ill-led, were confined to a position where their superior numbers were useless. It was a stunning victory, often viewed as the climax of the war, but it did not end the struggle for independence.

The Wars of Independence AD 1296–1329.

The Wars of Independence AD 1329–1357.

Kildrummy Castles held for David II after Halidon Hill

Land ceded to England by Edward Balliol

Edward's refusal to consider peace saw Scottish attacks intensify. A Scottish invasion undermined the English hold on Ireland and ended its role as a source of revenue and supplies. Despite raids which penetrated into Yorkshire, Edward refused to sue for peace. His overthrow in January 1327 broke the log-jam, but the peace remained unpopular in England: it was recognised that the war had ended in humiliation. Nevertheless, in 1328 the Treaty of Edinburgh was ratified and Robert achieved his objective of a Scotland free from overlordship. It was intended as a lasting peace, and reconciliation was sought through the marriage of Robert's heir, David, to Edward III's sister, Joan, but it left much unresolved. Nevertheless, when Robert died in June 1329, his kingdom was at peace, self-confident in its independence.

'WOE TO THEE, O LAND, WHOSE RULER IS A CHILD'

It has been said that rather than being born late (in 1324), it would have been better for Scotland had **David II** never been born at all. It is a harsh statement, but in view of the consequences of the accession of another minor, carries some justification. It was bad enough that a child had succeeded, auguring weak government, but he faced also an ambitious English king smarting from the terms of the 1328 treaty.

A vehicle for English ambitions lay in a group of nobles who claimed property in Scotland. They, known as the **Disinherited**, gathered around Edward Balliol, son of the former king. Edward III could not directly aid the Disinherited, but in 1332 he agreed secretly to support Balliol's bid for the Scottish throne. In August 1332, the Disinherited defeated the Scots at Dupplin near Perth, and in September Balliol was crowned king. Scotland now had rival kings and, testifying to lingering loyalties to the Balliol cause, civil war erupted once more. Nevertheless, before the end of 1332, David's supporters drove Balliol from Scotland.

Balliol's appeal to **Edward III** for aid brought an English army to Berwick in spring 1333. The Scots marched to relieve the town, but in July, at Halidon Hill, Edward's archers decimated their army. Defeat saw the collapse of resistance: only a handful of castles flew the Bruce standard. Balliol now repaid his debt to his overlord, ceding southern Scotland. So grave was the situation that in 1334 David was sent to France. Almost immediately, however, the Disinherited squabbled over the pickings, allowing the Scots to regain the initiative: by 1337 the country beyond the Forth had been recovered. By then, however, Edward III was losing interest in a war which was costly and which did not conform to his chivalric ideals. In October 1337 Edward laid claim to the throne of France, opening the Hundred Years War. For him, Scotland was a side issue.

In 1341 David returned from exile and began to reconstruct his government. Efforts to rein in magnates who had enjoyed the absence of supervision produced tension. Failure to check flagrant abuses of power provoked dissent among the Scots, and when in October 1346 David invaded England it was with a divided kingdom at his back. He did not, however, expect serious opposition: Edward III was in France, engaged on the siege of Calais. Victory would have given him the authority which Bannockburn had brought his father. But the Scots' plans were an open secret, and Edward had prepared his defences: his deputies presided over the destruction of David's army at Neville's Cross outside Durham and the capture of the king. His unexpected defeat had reversed a decade of unbroken Scottish success in the war against England.

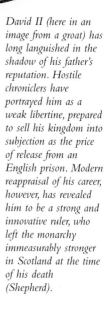

David II (here in an image from a groat) has long languished in the shadow of his father's reputation. Hostile chroniclers have portrayed him as a weak libertine, prepared to sell his kingdom into subjection as the price of release from an English prison. Modern reappraisal of his career, however, has revealed him to be a strong and innovative ruler, who left the monarchy immeasurably stronger in Scotland at the time of his death (Shepherd).

THE QUEST FOR LASTING PEACE

Neville's Cross was a savage blow, but, despite the the capture of David, it was not decisive. There was no follow up to the battle, and Robert Stewart, David's heir and lieutenant in his absence, controlled the heartland of the kingdom. The removal of the king, however, permitted Robert and other nobles to bolster their own position at

Building an image

From the time of Alexander II a clear impression can be gained of the use of architecture as a tool in royal image-making. There is no questioning the message implicit in castles such as Kildrummy, Aberdeenshire, built to control the routes from Strathdon into Moray: the scale and quality of materials proclaim the wealth, sophistication and inherent superiority of a monarchy which had united Scotland under its governance. David II understood the value of architecture in enhancing royal prestige in his rebuilding of crown authority after 1357. In 1366, work commenced on David's Tower at Edinburgh Castle (now encased in the Half Moon Battery see p. 25), an unequivocal projection of royal might, dominating the burgh below and symbolising David's grasp on power within his realm.

the expense of the Crown: government lapsed into chaos. Understandably, Robert showed little urgency to secure David's release, while Edward had little interest in opening ransom negotiations. Stalemate had been reached.

In 1348, Edward began negotiations, seeking to maximise on the strong position which possession of David afforded. The Scots, however, would not redeem their king at any price, and proposals which involved acceptance of overlordship were rejected. In the hope of winning French assistance, the Scots drew out discussions until 1355, but the capture of King Jean in 1356 brought them to the negotiating table.

Edward Balliol, for a substantial pay-off, resigned his rights to Edward, giving him a personal claim to the Scottish crown and negotiations revolved around this point. The Scots, however, would not discuss overlordship, and, without settlement of that issue, lasting peace was unobtainable. In October 1357, compromise was reached in the **Treaty of Berwick**: for a 100,000 merk ransom payable over 10 years, a truce for the duration, and surrender of 23 hostages, David was released. Edward expected future negotiations to bring the settlement he wanted, but the Scots had freed their king without making concessions on overlordship or the royal succession.

RECONSTRUCTION

From 1357 until his death in 1371, **David** concentrated on three issues: restoration of royal power; production of an heir; and lasting peace with England. The first he pursued with ruthless efficiency, clawing back powers usurped during his captivity, and recovering unpaid revenues. David needed money, not only to finance reconstruction of government, but also to pay his ransom. Through the appointment of able servants and a partnership with the influential and wealthy merchant-burgesses, David achieved a remarkable turnaround in his revenues.

David's reconstruction of royal authority used servants dependent on him for power and position. He had little reason to trust his traditional nobles, especially Robert Stewart, and set about curbing their powers and intruding his own men into positions of local power. Determination to re-establish royal supremacy antagonised the men who had enjoyed influence in his absence, and in 1363 he faced a rebellion. Its swift suppression underscored the scale of the royal recovery and David's abilities as king: by the end of 1363 he was undisputed master of Scotland.

The questions of an heir and peace with England were

interlinked. In 1357, David was 33 and childless, a problem compounded by Queen Joan's residence in England from 1358 until her death in 1362. David had mistresses, but as none became pregnant, rumours of infertility grew. Against this background, Edward proposed restoration of English-held lands, cancellation of the ransom, and guaranteed conservation of Scottish institutions and privileges, in return for his or his heir's succession to the Scottish throne should David die childless. David was prepared to gamble, but parliament rejected the proposals. Angered, Edward imposed a higher ransom, but, by 1369, to avoid Scottish involvement in a renewed French war, he reduced the ransom to its original level and offered a 14-year truce. This proved a final position, and when Edward died in 1377 English claims to overlordship had become an irrelevancy.

IACOBVS·I·D·GRAT[
REX·SCOTORVM

CHAPTER 3

OF MISFORTUNES AND MINORITIES

OPPOSITE: *James I is commonly portrayed as heralding a new beginning in Scottish history. His reign witnessed the aggressive reassertion of royal power after half a century of erosion yet he was ultimately a failed autocrat whose policies contributed to his death. Portrait by an unknown artist (by kind permission of The Scottish National Portrait Gallery).*

Althorugh the wars with England, which we charted in the last chapter, were never formally concluded by a final peace settlement, it was clear by the late 14th century that England's challenge to Scottish independence was a thing of the past.

THE FIRST STEWARTS

The accession of **Robert II** in 1371 marked a historical turning point. Peace with England provided the stability to secure Robert's grip on the throne. Soon, his sons were established in positions of power: by 1384 they controlled the earldoms of Caithness, Ross, Buchan, Atholl, Strathearn, Menteith, Fife and Carrick, and were linked by marriage to powerful families like the MacDonalds, Lindsays and Rosses. Family rivalries quickly emerged, with Robert's two eldest sons, John, Earl of Carrick, and Robert, Earl of Fife, at loggerheads with their younger brother, Alexander, Earl of **Buchan**, who had been chosen by his father to provide the strong government which the Highlands had lacked since the 1340s.

Commonly portrayed as a ditherer presiding over the decay of the monarchy built up by David II, recent reassessments have rehabilitated Robert II. Rather than a senile nonentity, Scotland had acquired a shrewd and manipulative ruler. Image drawn from a groat (Shepherd).

In 1384, **Carrick** used concern over Highland lawlessness as an excuse to seize executive power from his father. Carrick and his associates, moreover, favoured war with England, and overran Teviotdale and Annandale. In 1385 the English devastated Lothian, but Carrick remained defiant. This hastened his downfall, for in 1388 at Otterburn, his ally, James, Earl of Douglas, was killed. Douglas's death stripped Carrick of political support and, in December 1388, Carrick was relieved of his powers, supposedly on account of infirmity – he had been lamed by a kick from a horse – and failure to quell disorder in the Highlands.

1350	
DAVID II	
Accession of Stewarts	1371
ROBERT II	
Wolf of Badenoch burns Elgin Cathedral	1390
1400 **ROBERT III**	
James I - captured by English pirates	1406
JAMES 1	
Death of Duke of Albany	1420
Release of James from captivity in England	1424
	1437
JAMES II	
1450	
Destruction of Black Douglases	1455
Roxburgh retaken from English	1460
Treaty with Denmark -	1468
Scots gain Orkney (1468) & Shetland (1469)	
JAMES III	
Battle of Sauchieburn	1488
Forfeiture of Lordship of the Isles	1493
1500 **JAMES IV**	
James IV marries Margaret Tudor	1503
Battle of Flodden	1513
JAMES V	
Battle of Solway Moss	1542
Mary sent to France	1548
1550 **MARY**	
Reformation Parliament	1560
Mary returns from France	1561
Abdication of Mary	1567
Execution of Mary	1587
JAMES VI	
1600 *Accession of James VI to English throne*	1603
James plans sole visit to Scotland	1617
	1625
CHARLES I	

In his place, **Fife** was appointed lieutenant.

After his accession as **Robert III** in 1390, Carrick was deemed incapable of exercising government, and Fife's lieutenancy continued. In 1393, aided by his son, **David**, Earl of Carrick, Robert asserted his power, but by 1397 authority was slipping from him, with David becoming the real power behind the throne. A general council in 1398, which saw the creation of the honorific dukedoms of **Albany** and **Rothesay** for Fife and Carrick, voiced dissatisfaction with Robert's policies. In 1399 Rothesay, now allied with his uncle, Albany, was appointed lieutenant.

Rothesay's lieutenancy proved disastrous. Albany had hoped to rule through him, but Rothesay's independence threatened the political balance of the kingdom. As Rothesay's confidence mounted, Albany watched his influence slip away, and in 1401 he took decisive action. In a coup which used Rothesay's ungovernable character as a pretext for arrest, he was seized and taken to Falkland in Fife. Knowing that this had made a bitter enemy of the heir to the throne, Albany clearly saw only one course of action: in March 1402 it was announced that Rothesay was dead.

THE ALBANY GOVERNORSHIP

Robert held deep suspicions of his brother's part in Rothesay's death, but was in no position to act. With his remaining son, **James**, a boy of eight, there was no alternative to Albany as lieutenant. In 1406, as his health failed, Robert clearly feared for his son's future, and attempted to send James to France. The plan failed.

James's vessel was captured by English pirates and he was carried prisoner to London. News of this disaster proved fatal to the king, and on 4 April 1406 he died.

With James captive in England, Albany assumed the regency for his nephew. His rule saw diminution of royal power, since the policies which he pursued did not require interventionist government or rigorous collection of revenue. Foreign policy, too, was low-key, Albany's attitude towards England being influenced by the captivity there from 1402 of his son, Murdoch. There was little effort to secure the release of James. Indeed, Albany's priority was Murdoch's freedom. His release in 1416 presaged a stronger line towards England. In 1419 Albany's second son, John, Earl of Buchan, and Archibald, Earl of Douglas, led an expeditionary force to France. Buchan's victories, and English weakness after Henry V's death in 1422, led to a change in English attitudes towards the release of James. Scottish attitudes, too, changed following Albany's death in 1420 and his succession as governor by Murdoch. In 1424, after a captivity of 18 years, the Scots agreed to ransom James for £33,000 sterling, and surrendered 27 noble hostages as security: the Albany governorship was over.

Handicapped by injury and excluded from exercise of power by his ambitious younger brother, the reign of Robert III witnessed a steady decline in royal prestige. Aware of his own shortcomings, the king is recorded as having described himself as 'the worst of kings and most wretched of men in the whole kingdom'. Image drawn from a groat (Shepherd).

Doune Castle, Stirlingshire. Built by Robert Stewart, 1st Duke of Albany, its towering walls bear testimony to the ambitions of this most capable of Stewart princes. Located in the heart of his earldom of Menteith, it was the focus for a great complex of estates spread from Dumbarton to Atholl which formed the basis of Albany's power (Historic Scotland).

THE COVETOUS KING: JAMES I

James I inherited a near-bankrupt crown burdened with a large ransom. The solution lay in a clawback of alienated royal property, a move deeply unpopular amongst the nobles. His difficulties were eased by gains from Albany adherents: in 1424 when Buchan and Douglas were killed in France, Buchan's lands and offices fell to James and in 1425, when he executed Murdoch and his sons for treason, their forfeiture brought an enormous windfall to the crown.

James's chief concern was royal image-building and the creation of a monarchy which stood at the heart of national life. This saw forceful action taken against 'overmighty' subjects, a course which won the hearts of many people. The fall of the Albany Stewarts was followed by successful curbs on Douglas supremacy in the south. Attempts at similar action against the MacDonalds, however, rebounded, and by 1431 James agreed terms with the Lord of the Isles. Nevertheless, overall he succeeded in building an aura of invulnerability around the monarchy, and cultivated an exalted image of kingship. One manifestation of this was **Linlithgow**, built as the setting for a splendid court. Such projects placed a heavy drain on his resources, but in 1427 he defaulted on his ransom and abandoned the hostages. Amongst these was his cousin, Malise, Earl of Strathearn, whom James stripped of his wealthy earldom and awarded instead the much poorer Menteith. Such measures typified James's quest for finance, leading to mounting distrust of the king by his nobility.

Linlithgow Palace, West Lothian. Symbol of the ambitions of James I, Linlithgow was built as a formal projection of the king's aim to create a powerful new monarchy at the heart of his kingdom (Historic Scotland).

By 1436, cracks appeared in the image of invulnerability and James encountered criticism of increasingly autocratic policies. The humiliating failure of an expedition to retake Roxburgh shattered the illusion. In February 1437, a group of conspirators headed by Sir Robert Graham, a kinsman of Earl Malise, and acting with the connivance of the king's uncle, Atholl, ended what they saw as tyranny. On 21 February, while the king and queen were in Perth, the conspirators assassinated James.

JAMES II: THE KING WITH THE FYRE MARK IN HIS FACE

At the time of his father's murder, **James II** was only six. Atholl hoped to become lieutenant during the minority, but, with James secure in their hands, the council rounded up and executed the assassins. Atholl's complicity in the plot secured his execution, completing the elimination of the junior branches of the royal Stewarts.

This elimination of royal kinsmen produced a vacuum of power during the minority, filled by families of lesser rank like the Crichtons and the Livingstones; it ended only when James was declared of age in 1449. He then faced the task of restoring royal authority after years of erosion.

Marriage to **Mary of Gueldres** revealed how thoroughly royal revenues had been plundered since 1437: James struggled to provide the promised marriage portion. Royal financial difficulties fuelled political tensions between the Crown and the **Earl of Douglas**. Crisis erupted from an agreement between Douglas and the earls of Crawford and Ross, which James feared was directed against him. In 1453, when Douglas refused to break the bond, James stabbed him to death. Peace was patched up before the end of the year, but it was a sham: James was preparing for a decisive move. In 1455 he was ready, and in a rapid campaign shattered Douglas power, drove the new earl into exile, and seized the Douglas lands in the largest property windfall to the Crown since Bannockburn.

The destruction of the Douglases gave James unrivalled power. Master of his realm, he turned after 1455 to regaining the last English-controlled areas of Scotland. Careful preparations for war heralded a reopening of conflict. Civil war in England presented James with an unparalleled opportunity, and in July 1460, James encamped before the walls of Roxburgh. On 3 August, during a salvo to greet the arrival of the queen, a cannon exploded and the king, who was standing nearby, was killed. With his heir, now **James III**, only eight years old, Scotland faced another minority.

The 12-year minority at the start of the reign of James II saw the undermining of much of his father's work in building a strong monarchy. At the beginning of his personal rule in 1449, he showed determination to be his own man and to end the nobility's grip on power, best shown by his total destruction of the Black Douglases, the greatest of the noble kindreds. Image, showing the disfiguring fiery birth mark, drawn from an illumination by Jörg von Ehingen (Shepherd).

THE TYRANNOUS PRINCE: JAMES III

Another troubled minority ended in 1469 when James III took control of government and married Margaret, daughter of Christian I of Denmark. As pledge for her dowry, James received control of Orkney and Shetland, bringing Scotland to its maximum territorial extent.

James's exalted image of the monarchy was reflected through artistic patronage and broadcast through his introduction of new coins which bore a three-quarters portrait of the king, the first renaissance imagery of its kind north of the Alps. Image drawn from a groat of c. 1485 (Shepherd).

Continuing civil war meant that the English were in no position to benefit from the minority in Scotland. The Scots, indeed, pressed on and captured Roxburgh, and in 1461 regained Berwick. A truce with Edward IV of England in 1464 ended hostilities, leaving Scotland in possession of these last traces of Edward III's conquests.

At the end of his minority in 1469, ambitious to make his mark on the international scene and increase royal revenues, the 17 year-old **James III** presented parliament with schemes for overseas conquests: Brittany, Gueldres and Saintonge. Baulked in 1473 by parliamentary veto, James staged a remarkable policy shift and settled a treaty with England in 1474. This was followed by a dramatic assertion of power within Scotland, when in 1475, having been advised of a treasonable agreement between John, Lord of the Isles and Earl of Ross, and the English, he stripped him of Ross.

James, however, faced hostility amongst his subjects at large. At the root of his problems lay a cavalier attitude towards justice, and interference with the coinage, where the silver content was drastically reduced. Resentment, too, centred upon growing dependence on a narrow circle of court favourites who formulated royal policy. Attacks on his popular younger brothers, Alexander, Duke of Albany, and John, Earl of Mar, whom he suspected of plotting against him, led to the exile of Alexander and the death of John in suspicious circumstances, further adding to the king's unpopularity.

The crisis came to a head in 1482 when war with England reopened. The gathering of the Scottish army brought together James's opponents, and at Lauder they mounted a political coup. Having hanged James's favourites, the army abandoned its march to the relief of Berwick – which fell to the English – and returned to Edinburgh. James, though, survived the crisis and resumed his unpopular policies. By 1488, **opposition** found a figurehead in the heir, James, Duke of Rothesay, who became nominal leader of an insurrection against his father. The king attempted negotiation, but in June he took the field against the rebels. On 11 June 1488, the armies met at **Sauchieburn** near Stirling and the king's force was routed. The fleeing king was thrown from his horse and carried to a nearby cottage, where, shortly afterwards, he was stabbed to death by an unknown hand.

Lands and dependencies of the Lordship of the Isles

Land under English domination to c.1460

SHETLAND
(From Denmark - Norway 1469)

ORKNEY
(From Denmark - Norway 1468)

15th-century Scotland.

THE GOLDEN AGE RE-VISITED: JAMES IV

James III's overthrow was followed by a remarkable pulling together of the once divided political community of the kingdom. This unity, coupled with the young king's popularity, considerably enhanced the power of the Crown. The authority which James IV commanded allowed him to tackle disorder in peripheral zones, particularly in the Isles. Since 1475, there had been growing strife between John, Lord of the Isles, and his son, which disturbed the

The marriage of the Thistle and the Rose

By 1502, relations with England had improved, and a Treaty of Perpetual Peace between the kingdoms was settled, cemented in 1503 by the marriage of James to Margaret, daughter of Henry VII. This represented the pinnacle of James's success. Growing awareness of the stature of their king, the sense of well–being which his government engendered, and the artistic flowering under royal patronage, combined to produce a sense that this was a new golden age (Shepherd).

James IV was no mere figurehead for the nobles who destroyed his father. Even-handed policies restored stability to the realm, but James's exercise of government owed much to his father's concept of kingship. Portrait by an unknown artist (by kind permission of The Scottish National Portrait Gallery).

peace of the region. To end this, in 1493 James suppressed the Lordship. James's adventure in the Isles gave him a taste for war, and in 1496 he attacked England. Failure to achieve any significant advantage saw him abandon the venture, while English failure to launch retaliatory raids convinced him of his skill as a general. As a consequence, James continued to develop his armed forces, building warships and an artillery train, both of which he dreamed of leading against the Turks as commander of a new crusade.

After 1509, Anglo–Scottish relations again turned sour. Enmeshed in a complex of conflicting treaties – he was allied to both France and England – James was outmanoeuvred in the morass of European diplomacy. Playing on his idealism and crusading dreams, in 1512 the

pope commanded him to enter an alliance against France, while France promised aid against the Turks in return for an alliance against England and the papacy. When war erupted in 1513, James was caught between peace with England and alliance with France. Failed negotiations with England and the pope saw James lead his army into England in Autumn 1513. On 9 September, at **Flodden**, the king and the cream of his fighting men were slaughtered.

JAMES V: A VINDICTIVE KING

With the new king only 18 months old, Scotland faced a long minority. Fortunately, Henry VIII did not pursue the war, for he hoped to exercise influence in Scotland through his sister, Margaret, but her re-marriage in 1514 to Archibald Douglas, **Earl of Angus**, alienated many Scots. In 1515 they were driven from power when John, Duke of Albany, the king's cousin, arrived from France to become regent. His departure in 1524 saw Queen Margaret resume government in alliance with the Earl of Arran, but in 1526, following her divorce from Angus, her ex-husband staged a coup and seized the king. Until 1528, when James escaped from Angus's control, the earl ruled Scotland through possession of the king.

James V's personal rule saw rigorous reassertion of royal power. His actions, however, were tainted with vindictiveness, directed in particular against the wealthy amongst his nobility. His captivity instilled in him an intense hatred of the Douglas family, who paid heavily for James's forgiveness. Attacks on other men, however, often on trumped up charges, were aimed at seizure of their wealth for the Crown.

Aggressive government was matched by ambitious building and expensive diplomacy, which needed greater wealth than was obtainable from traditional sources available to James. His uncle, **Henry VIII**, urged him to follow his example and seize the immense wealth of the Church, but James preferred a more subtle approach. Using threats of Reform as a lever, he taxed the clergy heavily. This revenue was supposed to finance the College of Justice which James founded in 1531–32, but instead funded his extravagant court.

Scottish alignment with France was of grave concern to Henry VIII, and, when James married **Mary of Guise**, rapidly deteriorating relations eventually dissolved into war. James faced opposition at

Throughout the 1530s, James V was one of Europe's most eligible royal bachelors: Scottish military power was courted by the rival power blocs of the day. Proposals for marriage to a Tudor or Habsburg princess prompted Francis I of France to agree to the marriage of his daughter, Madeleine, to James. She survived only a few months, dying in July 1537, whereupon James immediately sought a new French bride, and in 1538, married Mary of Guise, of the powerful family of Guise-Lorraine. One of the wooden roundels from the ceiling of the Presence Chamber at Stirling Castle possibly depicting James (Historic Scotland)

home, and when his army entered England in November 1542 it was riven by dissent. News of its defeat at Solway Moss broke the king's health, and three weeks later, six days after the birth of his daughter, Mary, James died at Falkland.

ROUGH WOOINGS, REFORMATION AND REVOLUTION

James's death triggered a grave crisis, for **Mary** was just six days old. Furthermore, the kingdom was deeply divided, with religion souring traditional rivalries. There was increasing disenchantment with France, whom they felt had brought nothing but disaster to Scotland, and many believed instead that Scotland's future lay with England. Religion influenced these trends, with English aid in securing the Reform of the Church within Scotland being sought, while France offered succour for the harried establishment.

Mary the Queen

Queen of Scots at just six days old, Mary was, for all her life, a pawn in the complex game of European diplomacy. Ill-prepared to govern a kingdom wracked by religious and political dissent, she was eventually overwhelmed by those with a better grasp on the realities of power. Profile of Mary drawn from a gold ryal or £3-piece (Shepherd).

Henry VIII was hardly altruistic: a pro-English regime in Scotland was a desirable objective. Mary opened prospects of greater control for her marriage to Henry's son, the future Edward VI, would see the realisation of ancient English ambitions, the incorporation of Scotland into a greater English realm. **Solway Moss** provided Henry with a lever by which to further this plan: release of prisoners was conditional upon their support for the marriage. The Scottish regent, the Protestant James, Earl of Arran, agreed in July 1543 to the Treaty of Greenwich, which settled the marriage.

The treaty was stillborn. In autumn 1543, Cardinal Beaton of St Andrews, persuaded Arran to reconvert to Catholicism, repudiate the treaty, and ally with France. Baulked, Henry turned to intimidation to force through the marriage deal in the savage war of the 'Rough Wooing'. Lothian and the Borders were devastated, but the Scots refused to submit. War continued after Henry's death, and in September 1547, the English won a crushing victory at Pinkie near Edinburgh.

The arrival of French soldiers in June 1548 neutralised English war gains, and by the Treaty of Haddington, the Scots affirmed alignment with France. Under its terms, Mary went to France as the bride of the Dauphin, heir to the French throne: Mary's marriage brought regal union, but it was of Scotland and France, not Scotland and England.

From 1548, French influence in Scotland grew and in 1554 Mary of Guise assumed the regency. This secured French control of Scotland to counterbalance the marriage alliance of Queen Mary of England with France's Spanish enemies. The regent, however, was conciliatory towards the Reformers in a bid to win general approval, but England's return to Protestantism in 1558 revived fears of Protestant insurrection in Scotland, and Mary adopted a policy of repression. It was counterproductive and outraged moderate opinion. Soon, the regent's reliance on French officials for her government and French soldiers for her power alienated even staunchly Catholic lords.

Rebellion erupted in 1559, with many burghs appointing Protestant ministers to their churches to signal rejection of the regent's authority. In June 1560, Mary of Guise died: the Catholic and French cause in Scotland collapsed overnight. The following month, the Treaty of Leith saw the withdrawal of both English and French soldiers from Scotland and, left to themselves, in August 1560 parliament carried through legislation for **Reformation.**

St Andrews Castle, St Andrews, Fife. Under the leadership of David Beaton, Cardinal-Archbishop of St Andrews, the pro-French Catholic party in Scotland reasserted its control of government and overturned plans to marry Queen Mary to Henry VIII's son. Beaton's murder in May 1546 in his own castle by a group of Protestant Fife lairds tore apart the fragile peace between the religious factions in the kingdom (Oram).

THE RELUCTANT QUEEN

When **Mary** and her husband, **Francis,** ascended the throne as rulers of France and Scotland in July 1559, there seemed little prospect of her returning to her homeland, but Francis's death in December 1560 made return a certainty. For the Scots, who lacked a legally constituted government, her return was imperative, but Mary showed great reluctance. The people, too, were wary: raised as a Catholic, how would the Queen react to the Reformation settlement? Eventually, after a delay of eight months in which she tried to find a suitable husband amongst European royal houses, she sailed for home.

Mary was greeted with rapture, but her arrival in August 1561 produced an atmosphere of uneasiness. Catholics expected the overturning of the Reformation, while Protestants demanded that she ratify the acts of

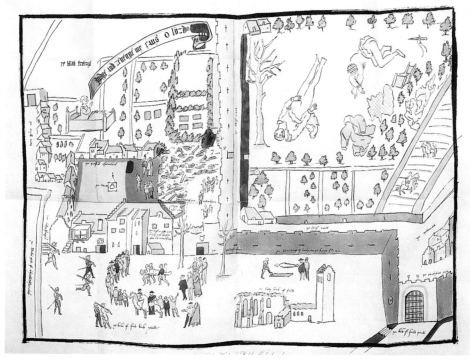

The Murder of Darnley: 19th-century facsimilie of the drawing illustrating a report of Darnley's murder sent to the English authorities.
In 1566, Darnley had joined a plot to murder Mary's Italian secretary, David Rizzio, an act for which she never forgave him. After a brief reconciliation and the birth of their son, their relationship again broke down: in February 1567, Darnley was assassinated at Kirk o' Field in Edinburgh.

the 1560 parliament: she did neither. This failure to act decisively set the character of her reign, and ensured that she never established a grip on her own government. Policy, instead, was directed by her half–brother, **Lord James Stewart**, and a Protestant dominated council. Their priority was for good relations with England, especially since Mary, as the closest living relative of **Elizabeth I**, seemed likely to succeed the childless English queen. After the death of Francis, it was essential that any new husband for Mary should be acceptable to Elizabeth: her marriage to her cousin, Henry Stewart, **Lord Darnley**, angered the English queen and proved ultimately disastrous for Mary.

The stormy marriage ended in Darnley's violent death in circumstances which are still subject to debate. Contemporary opinion blamed the Earl of **Bothwell.** Mary, too, was suspected, and when in May 1567 she married Bothwell, she destroyed her reputation and precipitated civil war. Defeated by her rebellious lords, Mary surrendered, was forced to abdicate in favour of her son and imprisoned. In 1568 she escaped and attempted to regain the throne, but on the defeat of her army, fled south and threw herself on the mercy of Elizabeth I. It was a grave miscalculation, leading to 19 years of imprisonment and finally execution in 1587.

THE STEWARTS TRIUMPHANT

Mary's defeat did not end the civil war: until 1573 her supporters fought on in her name. Possession of **James VI** strengthened her opponents, who ensured that he was raised as a Protestant, and under a succession of Protestant regents the process of Reformation was pursued. James's education was entrusted to **George Buchanan**, a staunch Protestant, virulently hostile to Mary. From him, James acquired the intellectual tools which later won him a scholarly reputation, but Buchanan failed to indoctrinate him into passive acceptance of theories of limitations on kingship of which he was a passionate proponent.

In 1578, when James was 12, the last of his regents fell from power. In his place, various factions sought to control the king, the ultra-Protestant Earl of Gowrie even resorting to kidnap in 1582. James's escape in 1583 led to Gowrie's execution, and was followed by legislation against more radical Reforming elements, including in 1584 a declaration of royal supremacy over the Church. This was but the opening gambit in a protracted struggle between King and Kirk.

Reconstruction of the birth of James VI at Edinburgh Castle (Historic Scotland).

Baptism of James VI at the Chapel Royal, Stirling Castle (Historic Scotland).

James' Church reforms

Control of the Church was central to his beliefs, and James VI worked towards establishment of an Episcopalian system as a means of tightening his grip. Royally appointed bishops not only enforced conformity with James's will in the Church, but added to royal control over the council in which they sat. Royal power was further enhanced by James's creation of new nobles, men who made a career in royal service and depended on royal favour for their position. Such men formed a political elite which gave James unquestioned control over government and provided him with an authority unknown to his ancestors.

James's assertion of power was followed by reconciliation, the so-called 'middle way'. Moderation, however, did not imply weakness, and in a series of scholarly works James articulated a thesis which emphasised royal supremacy and the God-given nature of royal authority, a thesis which he intended to put into practice.

It was not until 1596 that James truly established control over the factions within the kingdom. **Religion** figured large in his legislation, but his primary concern was reimposition of authority in remote regions and in securing the Crown's financial position. The Highlands, Islands, and the Borders experienced rigorous action against disorder, the last being viewed as a priority since James was keen to maintain good relations with England: Border lawlessness might jeopardise his inheritance of Elizabeth's throne.

UNION

In March 1603, Elizabeth of England died. Less than two weeks later James left Scotland to assume power in his new kingdom. Behind him he left a Scotland vastly different from the land ruled by his ancestors, where royal government, exercised by a council of loyal

Crown servants, could function without the king's presence. From London, James continued to direct policy. Dissenters and radicals within the Church were removed, summoned to London and imprisoned. In 1610, James reintroduced a full Episcopalian system to Scotland, but further tinkering faced mounting opposition. In 1617, on his sole return visit, celebrations were tempered by hostility to his religious policies, but by 1621 he had carried through his plans. James's handling of this, and of efforts to impose new taxes, however, were less deft than his dealings with the Scots before 1603: his absence had blunted his perception of the political climate. It was success, too, at a price, for his son's inept handling of the same issues in the 1630s sparked an eruption of hostility which cost him his head.

It is James's death in 1625 that marks the end of our story, not his accession to the English throne in 1603. While Scotland was never the same after the Union of the Crowns, the policies which James's government pursued were continuations of trends set in motion in the 1590s. The experiences of his youth moulded his outlook on government, and he possessed a lifetime awareness of the problems of controlling Scotland, even though this awareness became blunted after 22 years in England. The accession of his son, **Charles I**, however, marked a radical new departure, for, although born in Scotland, by his education and experience he was English. Although technically he and his successors were kings and queens of Scotland and of England until 1707, the distinctive Scottishness of the monarchy died with James VI.

Made king by a revolution against his mother, James VI was educated by men who believed sincerely in the right of subjects to dethrone a tyrannous ruler. Their propaganda appeared even in the coins minted in the boy-king's name. Here, in an image from a groat, a Godly hand points towards a sword and the chilling message pro me si mereor in me *('For me, or in me if I deserve it') warns James of the fate in store for him if he rules unjustly (Shepherd).*

MALCOLVVS dei gra rex scottor Omnibz hoibz suis francis & anglis & scottis cunctisq: scē dei eccłe filiis: ꝑpetuā
salutem. Nouerint om̄s ꝉntes & futuri pie memorie auū regem scottor dm̄ meum, dum comes sui·fundasse
quandam abbatiam apud Seleschirche. in honore scē dei genitricis uirginis marie. & scī iohīs euangeliste
pro salute anime sue·& patris & matris sue·fratrq: & soror suarum·omniumq: antecessor successorq: suor.
Sꝫ postqm diuina clemencia post obitum fris sui in regnum·ei successit in regnum: consilio & ammonitōe
uenerabił memorie iohīs tc glascuensis epī·& ꝑcerū suor dm̄ consensu: predictam abbatiam. qua
locus ille non erat conueniens abbatie·apud rokesburgā transtulit in ecclām beate marie uirginis. que
sita ē sup ripam flumīs tuede. in loco qui dr kelcho. Quam ecclām ROBERTVS tc scī ANDR. in ea erat epc·ꝑ dei amore & suo·ab om̄i episco-
pali subiectione liberā ē concessit. Ita scilicet ut abbas & monachi supradicte eccłe·a quocūq: epo uoluerint. in scotia·uel in cumbria·crisma suum
& oleum·& ordinationem ipsi abbas & monachi·& eccła scē dei sacramenta accipiant. Hanc libertatem cum aliis libtatib3 & possessionibz quas ex libali-
tate duor meor regum ꝉł·patris mei comitis henrici·siue mea·possident: eis quantum ad me ꝑtinet·in ꝑpetuum concedo·& potestate regia in ꝑpetuam
elemosinam confirmo. Videlicet uillam de kelcho cum suis rectis diuisis·in terris & in aquis·solutam & quietam·& ab omni exactione libam·& qua-
dam terram quam de kotvls dedit iuxta diuisas ipsi uille·que ita descendit iuxam qua iter ad netkanes thyrn. & ad quietienceuos in ipsa eccła
insolleunicata. uel in alia diebz ferialibz in audtoro omnes offendatis meas. & omnium qui mecum erunt ipsi eccłe confirmo. Et in euen̄hc
...

[Body continues with numerous grants of lands, mills, fisheries, churches and tithes, in heavily abbreviated Latin, not fully legible.]

... HIS TESTIBVS· HERBERTO glasc epo· Willo morauiensi epo· GREg epo de dunkeld· Willo
cancellario· Robtio pote scī ANDR· matheo archidiacono· scī ANDR· ... Ricardo camerario· Nichol clico· Ric capelło· Magistro andr·
... comite· ferteth comite· Duncan com· Gillebrid com de argal· ...

ACTVM · APVD · ROKESBVRG

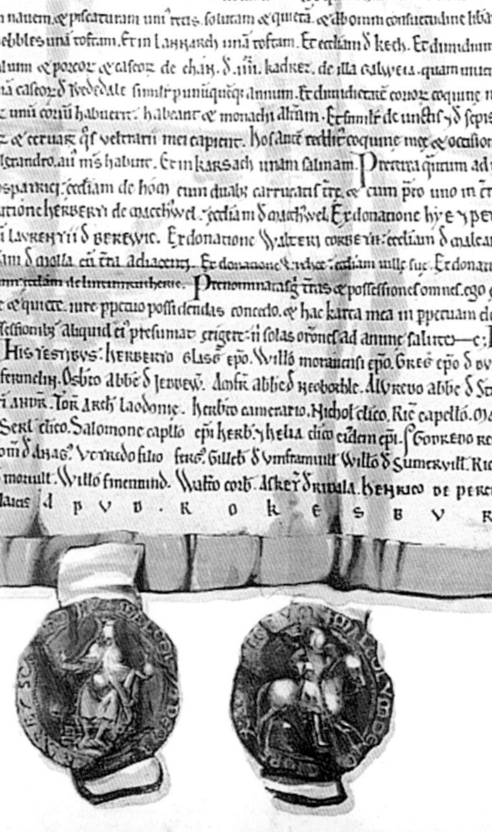

CHAPTER 4

GOVERNMENT, HOUSEHOLD AND ROYAL ADMINISTRATION

We have charted the political development of the kingdom of the Scots and the careers of its rulers, tracing the growth of the realm from its union of the Pictish and Scottish kingdoms down to the accession of Scotland's James VI to the English throne.

We now look more widely at the forces which enabled the rulers to create and sustain the kingdom. The success of the Scottish kings lay in a series of partnerships – with the Church, the nobility, the townsfolk – and their ability to construct a flexible system of government which could operate within the framework of these partnerships. Here, at the end of the 20th century, to talk of 'government' is to invoke images of legions of faceless bureaucrats, of Parliament, political parties, Prime Ministers and Cabinets. This system, however, was very much an 18th-century English development, far removed from the traditions of medieval and early modern Scotland. In contrast to the intensive government which underpinned the power of the kings of England, Scotland was lightly burdened with government and developed its own approaches to the management of the realm.

THE GROWTH OF ROYAL POWER

Scotland's government in the Middle Ages is often compared unfavourably with that of England. There, Crown authority was backed by the power of parchment-producing clerks, who

OPPOSITE: Malcolm IV's great charter to Kelso Abbey, c. 1159 (from a 19th-century facsimile). This charter bears striking witness to the parchment-based revolution in royal government set in motion by David I and his successors. Produced as a written confirmation, sealed by the king, of the abbey's lands, rights and privileges, it is the finest example surviving from the 12th century of the scribal art.

Cawdor Castle, Nairn. The most famous – or infamous – of all thanages, immortalised in Shakespeare's Macbeth. *Shakespeare's presentation of the thanes as Scotland's equivalent to the English earl is wide of the mark, for these were lowly administrators entrusted with the running of royal estates rather than great lords in their own right. The impressive 15th-century tower at the core of the present castle belongs to an age when Cawdor's lords had long established their hereditary title to the thanage (Oram).*

transmitted the royal will to the localities and brought uniform approaches to administration throughout the kingdom. Such government, too, was supported by regular taxation. Delegation of power to sheriffs, men entirely dependent on the king for their position, enabled the rapid implementation of instructions, which eased the exercise of justice and collection of revenue. There were dangers inherent in a system which concentrated such power in the king's hands, with only a narrow division between firm government and tyranny, but a counterbalance to royal demands developed in the form of parliament. Strong monarchy exercising intensive government, but regulated by parliament, then, is viewed as the ideal against which the shortcomings of others are gauged.

Scottish government seems to lack these attributes. From the early Middle Ages we gain an impression of kingship dependent on the personal ability of the ruler, where the king needed the co-operation of provincial rulers who enjoyed almost royal authority. Of course, the difficulties of a country as geographically divided and as culturally diverse as Scotland required flexibility of approach, and

there was little prospect of success for the rigid enforcement of uniformity by a remote ruler: power had to be delegated. Almost the only function other than supreme war leader in which the king exercised a national role was the making of laws, a tradition established as early as 858–862 when Donald I issued the laws of the Scots at Forteviot. Without a coinage controlled by the king, Scotland before 1150 could not develop a system of taxation capable of financing the extension of royal government; the Crown instead relied on traditional renders of produce for its support. There appeared no need for a bureaucracy to keep records of assessment and collection, and, where power was delegated to provincial rulers, there was little need for a writing office producing a flow of parchment instructions and enforcing administrative conformity.

AN ADMINISTRATIVE REVOLUTION

Signs of greater sophistication emerge in the 11th century. Throughout much of eastern Scotland from the Moray Firth to the Tweed there are traces of a network of **royal estates** administered for the king by a class of men referred to as **thanes**. Their duties involved the smooth running of the estate entrusted to their care, and the collection of dues from its inhabitants, much in the manner of the similar class in England who probably formed the model for the Scottish group. It was not, however, anything like a regular system, and it clearly developed in a haphazard fashion over time.

The reign of David I witnessed an administrative revolution. He had experience of the workings of English government and understood how it strengthened royal authority. As king, David introduced English techniques to Scotland, and began the development of a structured system of government. He still relied on the co-operation of the earls and lords for the enforcement of his will, but he introduced administrative shires controlled by **sheriffs** who had responsibility for local exercise of justice, maintenance of order, implementation of royal instructions and collections of dues. **Record keeping** became an essential tool for establishing royal power as the king started to define relationships between himself and his nobles, their duties and responsibilities, and the dues owed to him. Records were necessary for administration of justice, listing penalties imposed or payment of fines, so allowing the king to regulate the actions of his sheriffs. Written instructions flowed from the king to his agents, many being adaptations of forms developed in England, such as writs and brieves, marking an increased level of supervision and determination to ensure subservience to the royal will.

The Chapel

It is wrong to think of the Chapel (p. 62) as an institution like the Chancery in England. It was not in any fixed location, unlike its English counterpart which had settled at Westminster, but moved with the king. After all, these were his chaplains. Also, it was a small group whose primary duties were administration of the royal household, and accompanied the king's travels around the country. This was a mobile office, and records of where documents were issued show that it accompanied the king to the remotest corners of the land. The records themselves, however, soon became too bulky to be moved and a royal archive was established at Edinburgh.

*Arbroath Abbey, seat of Abbot Bernard, Chancellor of Robert I. Bernard was associated with the Bruce cause from the early days of Robert's bid for power. In 1311 he was made Abbot of Arbroath, and elevated in 1328 to the Bishopric of the Isles. In 1320 a letter, now known as the **Declaration of Arbroath**, was composed and sent to the pope – the most powerful expression of Scottish nationalism to come down from the Middle Ages (Oram).*

CHANCELLORS AND CHAPLAINS

This bureaucracy required literate clerks to staff the writing office which produced the tide of parchment which underpinned the new system. David and his successors drew their clerks from the clergy. Indeed, the king's chaplains fulfilled a dual role as priests and secretaries, and in Scotland the writing office where the documents were produced was known as the Chapel. The chief clerk held the office of **Chancellor**, who supervised the production of records and the authentication of documents, especially charters which recorded gifts of land and privileges, or royal letters, by use of the Great Seal. It was a post of great responsibility and prestige, and its holders expected to be rewarded with high office in the Church. Many became bishops or abbots. In the later Middle Ages the chancellor held great political influence and the kings awarded the title to already powerful men, not only to bishops or archbishops, but also to earls and lords.

Great Seal of Robert I. From the late 11th century the Great Seal – the principal seal used by the king – was used as the chief means of authenticating Crown charters and royal letters patent. Documents carrying this seal carried the full weight of royal authority (Shepherd).

Decentralised government, with power delegated into the hands of the nobility, did not require an elaborate bureaucracy. The dispersed and smaller population of the country, too, did not lend itself to intensive oversight in the English manner. Scottish government seemed rudimentary in comparison, but it worked and met the requirement of Scotland's rulers. It did become more sophisticated over time, but it was not until the 15th century that the output of the writing office expanded to such a level that it was impractical for it to remain mobile. Then the main department settled in **Edinburgh**, drawing up formal versions of documents from drafts and authenticating them with the Great Seal, enrolling charters in a formal register, and compiling the financial records. The king, however, still required a secretary to accompany him wherever he travelled, to deal with urgent correspondence and to produce drafts to be sent to Edinburgh. This personal writing office began to issue more formal documents, often to speed up business which might otherwise have become bogged down in the chancellor's office, and authenticated them with the king's Privy (secret) Seal instead of the Great Seal.

LEGAL AIDES

The expansion of royal authority in Scotland in the 12th century witnessed a range of measures designed to ease the burden. Amongst the king's most pressing business was administration of justice, but, as he reserved more aspects of jurisdiction to himself, there was a danger that he would be overwhelmed. Sheriffs acted as local judges with limited powers, and the earls and greater lords exercised extensive jurisdictions within their territories, but the king heard appeals or cases beyond the competence of the local courts, or involving crimes reserved for trial in the king's court. In the course of his travels around the kingdom, the king sat in judgement on cases brought before him, but by the middle of the 12th century the volume of business was outstripping his ability to respond in person.

Delegation was the answer. The arrangements for the exercise of justice in the absence of kings who divided their time between England and their Continental domains provided an example, and by around 1150 the Scots had introduced the office of **justice** or **justiciar**. This was a legal officer who deputised for the king, hearing classes of business beyond the competence of the sheriffs. A formal system emerged by the early 13th century, with **chief justices** exercising jurisdiction over defined areas. They were often major nobles, reflecting the prestige attached to the office. The most important justiciarate was **'Scotia'**, representing the core of the kingdom north of the Forth. Separate justiciarates for **Lothian** and **Galloway** were on record by 1221 and 1258 respectively.

Effigy of Alexander Stewart, son of Robert II, Lord of Badenoch and Justiciar of Scotia, from his tomb in Dunkeld Cathedral, Perthshire (Oram).

The **justiciarate** bestowed great influence on its holders. In periods of weak kingship, control of the office was hotly contested, as during the minority of Alexander III when Alan Durward and Walter Comyn struggled for political dominance, for they were powerful tools with which to influence local and national government. Once the king attained his majority, however, the justiciars were subordinated to an active monarch and their role reverted to that of judicial deputy rather than head of government.

The later 13th and 14th centuries witnessed a decline in the power of the justice. The reigns of Robert I and David II in particular saw trends towards grants of what is known as **regality** to the holders of earldoms and lordships. In effect, the king was delegating judicial powers, reserving only the four capital pleas of treason, murder, arson and rape for his own courts, although occasionally the right to try even these was ceded. Such grants diminished the scope of the justiciars, and as a consequence reduced their status.

Under the early Stewart kings the justiciarates acquired renewed significance. In the Highlands, the extinction of the Randolphs of Moray and the disintegration of their earldom created a power vacuum. Into this Robert II placed his son, Alexander, **Lord of Badenoch**, whom he built up as royal deputy in the north. Robert appointed Alexander to the justiciarate north of Forth, placing great political influence in the hands of one man. Alexander's power attracted the envy of his brothers, and he came under sustained attack in the late 1380s. The grant of the justiciarate to Alexander was intended to provide him with the authority to impose order on a region which had lacked firm government since the 1340s, but he was ill–suited to the responsibilities of office and in 1388 was charged with mismanagement and stripped of office.

COUNTING THE COSTS OF GOVERNMENT

A second office of great political influence was that of **royal chamberlain**. This post was amongst those introduced in the course

Robert Stewart, Earl of Fife and 1st Duke of Albany. Control of offices, such as the Chamberlainship, and the revenues attached to them added greatly to Albany's ability to maintain his hold over Scottish government. Image taken from William Hole's Frieze of Famous Scots *(reproduced by kind permission of The Scottish National Portrait Gallery).*

of the Normanisation of the royal household in the 12th century. The chamberlain was the king's chief financial officer and also supervised the affairs of the royal burghs. Oversight of the king's finances gave the chamberlainship great influence and it, like the justiciarates, was a coveted post.

With the appointment of Robert II's son-in-law, **John Lyon**, to the post, the chamberlainship became a dignity to be conferred on favoured individuals rather than an active administrative post, with much of the workload carried by deputies. The salary attached to the post made it attractive despite its declining status, and possession was secured by Robert, Earl of Fife. Under him, the chamberlainship continued to decline in importance, with deputies assuming real responsibility. James I, after his return to Scotland in 1424, completed its eclipse. Although the post remained in existence until 1705, James stripped it of power and divided its responsibilities between two new dignitaries, the treasurer and the comptroller. Henceforward, no one man had oversight of the royal finances.

COUNCILS AND COLLOQUIA

Much of the power of the royal household officials stemmed from attendance on the king. His **advisers** formed the core of his mobile household, and lists of witnesses attached to royal charters show how restricted this group was. In the 12th century, it was not uncommon for a narrow circle composed of the chancellor, chamberlain, **steward** (the man responsible for the domestic running of the household) and **constable** (responsible for the security of the court), padded out by household knights and royal clerks, to be in regular attendance on the king. Their ranks were swollen at major state occasions, but for most bishops, earls and great lords, their regular duties precluded long term residence at court. Essentially, therefore, a restricted household group formed the **king's council**.

In their running of the realm, Scotland's rulers took advice from their council: royal decisions were not arbitrary autocratic decrees. Advice on specialist matters would be sought from the appropriate officer – justiciars, chamberlain, chancellor, and so on – with the chancellor, by virtue of the powers which he enjoyed as keeper of the Great Seal, being the head of the council. The council should be seen more as an executive arm of government, with a competence that embraced most aspects of the running of the kingdom. It may seem a rather *ad hoc* arrangement in comparison to the bureaucracies of modern governments, but it was adequate for the rulers of the day.

Affairs of state, such as the making of foreign treaties, preparations

The post of Chamberlain

A competent chamberlain was essential for the smooth running of the administration, demonstrated in particular in the reign of David II. After years of civil and foreign wars, collection of revenue had fallen into arrears and many noblemen collected royal dues for their own ends. David appointed skilled servants to the post of chamberlain, and the success of William Bullock, appointed in 1341, was astounding. He reduced an accumulated deficit of nearly £3000 to just under £2 by 1342, but it won the bitter enmity of many lords: Bullock was accused of treason and died in prison. More spectacular success was achieved by Walter Biggar, chamberlain from 1359 to 1376, who, by 1362, had achieved a surplus of over £4500 in royal expenditure.

The King's Presence Chamber, Stirling Castle. While the great business of state came to be decided increasingly through consultation, receiving petitions, granting of offices and the dispensation of patronage remained very much royal activities. Formal access to the monarch was a carefully regulated and highly ceremonial affair, conducted in a suite of prestigious chambers to enhance the aura of majesty around the royal person (Historic Scotland).

for war, or important legislation, required wider consent than was offered by this narrow body. By the 13th century, the important offices were held by men who occupied powerful places in society. For example, the chancellor was commonly bishop of one of the greater dioceses, such as Glasgow or St Andrews; the constableship became the hereditary office of the Comyn earls of Buchan. Such men could claim to represent wider interests, but it was common for the king to summon his principal tenants to advise him, producing a broad range of opinion from the greatest bishops and earls to the more important knights.

Meetings of this general council were referred to as **colloquia,** the equivalent Latin term for the Norman–French **parlement** of contemporary England. These colloquia, or **parliaments**, were summoned when the king felt it necessary to consult his wider nobility, but the element of consultation should not obscure the fact that the ruler decided who would be attend the meeting and what business would be discussed: this was not parliamentary democracy in the modern sense. Parliament dealt with business of widely varying types: in 1258–1259 it settled the factional disputes between the Comyns and Alan Durward; meetings in 1356–1357 discussed the peace with England; in 1437 it met to try the assassins of James I; in 1560 it carried through legislation which officially turned Scotland into a Protestant country.

Parliament's role developed in the 14th century as the Bruce kings undertook the reconstruction of the kingdom. Robert I involved parliament in decisions of state to secure broad support for his aims, and to present an appearance of unity abroad. Parliament ratified his plans for the prosecution of war with England; for redistribution of lands of forfeited traitors; for arrangements for government in his absence in Ireland. Most importantly, he gained parliament's approval for his plans for the **succession** to the throne should he die without a male heir.

David II's reign saw a major advance in parliament's role. In an effort to ensure that responsibility for the negotiations for peace with England and the release of the captive king was shared by all influential groups in the kingdom, in 1357 representatives of the main **burghs**, the **burgesses**, were summoned for the first time. Their economic power had long been recognised, but until that date they had no political voice. Henceforward they emerge as increasingly influential. David II underpinned the financial success of his reign through co-operation with the burgesses, and the parliaments of the 1360s saw much business concerned with their mercantile interests in particular. Of course, the burgesses represented the interests of only the narrow group which controlled the internal affairs of their community, and should not be seen as MPs acting on behalf of the general population. The Crown was simply consulting only those whose political or economic influence demanded attention.

Parliament was no toothless talking shop. Even David II, at the height of his power, could not take its decisions for granted, and in 1364 saw it reject proposals for a peace with England which might have compromised the kingdom's future independence, while in 1370 it legislated against royal actions which ran contrary to the law. Under the early Stewarts, assemblies voiced criticism of Crown policies and aided the various factions headed by Robert II's sons to make their bids for power. It was on parliamentary authority that Robert, Earl of Fife, exercised the lieutenancy for his father and brother down to 1399, and it was with parliament's approval that he was replaced by David, Duke of Rothesay.

Burgess Power. The burgh market (here at Broad Street in Stirling) was symbolic of the growing wealth and commercial power of the merchant burgesses. The Crown's need for cash support finally brought a political voice to this influential group in the 14th century, when Robert I and David II courted the merchants, seeking their financial support and in return, the granting the burgesses a place in parliament (Oram).

Despite such actions, parliament exercised little real power over the Crown. After all, it could not assemble without royal permission and there was no obligation on the king to summon regular parliaments. At times of crisis, where opposition to the monarch might be expected, parliament could be rigged by issuing summonses to men most likely to be sympathetic to the Crown's stance, as happened in the 1450s during James II's attack on the Black Douglases. Parliament, too, could be summoned simply to rubber–stamp legislation, most of which in any case was drafted by the king's advisers.

The first 'men in grey suits'

In the course of the 15th century, Scotland's rulers relied on a circle of advisers to frame and direct its policies. This group, known from the 16th century as the **Privy Council**, drew on the skills of the officers of state, and influential members of the clergy and nobility. Membership was a clear sign of who was in favour at any given time, but the Crown generally recognised the dangers of excluding powerful opponents: better to harness their power within the council. The influence normally enjoyed by royal councillors was revealed in James III's reign. In the 1470s, James depended increasingly on the advice of court favourites, who became the formulators of policy while council and parliament simply put those policies into effect. The official councillors became mere administrators frozen out of the exercise of real power. This produced resentment, fuelled by James's exclusion of powerful men from membership of even this weakened council. The result was a succession of rebellions, the last of which in 1488 ended in James's death.

The reign of James IV saw the restoration of the council to its central place in the moulding of **royal policy**. It came increasingly to oversee the workings of government, which gave its members great power during the minorities of the 16th century. It was essential that the ruler retain firm control of the council, as there was a danger that powerful factions could gain a dominant position through membership and effectively 'run' the ruler. This happened in Mary's reign, where the queen rarely attended meetings and the bulk of business before it did not originate with her. The result was a Protestant-dominated council which was able to consolidate its position at the expense of the Catholics. Mary's lack of control over her own government is revealed dramatically in the fact that in the revolt of 1567 which toppled her from the throne, almost all of her councillors were ranged against her.

Her son, James VI, stands in sharp contrast. Once he attained power in the late 1580s, James was a diligent attender of council and controlled its membership. Under his guidance, the Privy Council became the core of government, pliant to his will but capable of independent action. James's domination of his council enabled him to continue the remote government of Scotland from Whitehall after his accession to the English throne in 1603. His success was based largely on selection of career civil servants, men who were entirely dependent on the king for advancement: James had made them, he could as effectively break them. With an efficient council working for him, James could with some honesty boast that he ruled with the pen where his predecessors had scarcely been able to rule with the sword.

James VI's success depended on his grasp of the politics of Scotland and his choice of men of ability to govern the kingdom in his name. His son, Charles I, showed remarkable incompetence on both counts. His unwillingness to listen to advice alienated the ageing ministers inherited from his father, who in turn became obstructive and unresponsive. More worrying for the future was his reliance on the favourites at his English court, most often men who were out of touch with Scotland, such as William Alexander, Earl of Stirling, appointed in 1626 to the secretaryship of the council. He had spent most of his adult life out of Scotland and lacked the talent or political weight to control the wily old men who had served James VI so well. He was not the worst: Robert Maxwell, Earl of Nithsdale, could not enter the kingdom due to actions raised against him for debt. With such personnel, it is no surprise that the problems posed by an absentee and unsympathetic king, where the nobility were unable to apply traditional restraints on royal policy through either parliament or council, should erupt into a rebellion which almost destroyed the monarchy.

OPPOSITE: *Three 'men in grey suits': top, James Douglas, 4th Earl of Morton, regent from 1572–1578 but executed for his part in Darnley's murder; middle, George Buchanan, poet and philosopher, a supporter of Mary but ultimately to denounce her for her part in Darnley's murder; bottom, James Stewart, Earl of Moray, Mary Queen of Scots' half-brother and adviser; assassinated 1571. All drawn from contemporary portraits by unknown artists (Shepherd).*

CHAPTER 5

PIETY AND POLITICS

Amongst the recurrent themes in the story of Scotland's monarchs is that of the partnership forged between clergy and Crown. From the 6th century, when St Columba ordained Aedhan mac Gabhrain king of Dalriada, until the 16th, when the Catholic Mary found herself at odds with the Protestant lords, Scotland's rulers enjoyed a close relationship with the national Church.

CROWN–CHURCH RELATIONS IN THE MIDDLE AGES

Kings were the protectors and patrons of the fledgling Church, providing it with the stability and security which fostered and encouraged growth. In return, kings received the sanction of the clergy, a stamp of approval which gave new power and authority to rulers. It was a relationship maintained for mutual advantage, but over time it enriched the kingdom immeasurably, both spiritually and materially, and transformed the image of kingship.

Laconic chronicle entries and fragmentary survival of early records make it difficult to gain a detailed impression of the personal beliefs of the early kings of Scots or the Picts. Notices of royal support for individual holy men, the veneration of the relics of particular saints, or the foundation of monasteries, show that these kings carried personal religious convictions that were as deep as their obsessive desire for military glory, but it was military capability rather than personal piety that made or broke rulers. Church support for one royal candidate over another had often more to do with the dynastic loyalties of influential clerics than with the suitability of rivals for the kingship. Columba's ordination of Aedhan was a question of political realities, designed as much to further the interests of his Irish kinsmen as to safeguard the Church of **Iona.** It

OPPOSITE: *Glasgow Cathedral, St Kentigern's Shrine. Pilgrimages to the shrines of Scotland's national saints occupied a central position in the mix of piety and politics which formed the public face of royal religious devotions (Oram).*

Iona Abbey, Argyll. Columba's monastery on this remote Hebridean island symbolised the interdependence of politics and religion in early Scotland. The saint and his successors were kingmakers par excellence, while in turn the early kings of Scots protected the fledgling Christian mission and later aided the spread of its influence throughout the land (Shepherd).

had the effect, however, of enhancing the prestige of Aedhan and his descendants, and the Church could look in return for the active support of these kings.

Political expediency rather than piety dominated the relationship between clergy and kings for centuries. Controversies, such as that over the calculation of the date of Easter between supporters of the Roman system and the defenders of the older method prevalent in the Celtic west, carried deep political significance. Although masked by theological arguments, the decision of the Pictish king, **Nechtan,** to adopt the Roman usage in 711 stemmed from defeat at the hands of the Northumbrians and their re-establishment of overlordship of his kingdom rather than from pious motives.

THE RISE OF CHRISTIAN KINGSHIP

Piety could play a strongly political role. By the 9th century, sophisticated ideas of Christian kingship were circulating in Europe, springing largely from the revival of the Roman Empire in the West under **Charlemagne.** The image of the Christian king and the cult of kingship which it fostered were enthusiastically taken up and used to enhance the prestige of the king of the Picts and Scots. The naming of Pictish and Scottish kings after Constantine, the first Christian emperor, carried a powerful message. Certainly, the first of these, **Constantine son of Fergus**, was portrayed as protector and renewer of the Church: it was in his reign that the new ecclesiastical centre at **Dunkeld**, the spiritual successor of Iona, was founded. This image of the pious king, the founder of monasteries and churches, the renewer of the Christian life of his people as cast in the mould of the Emperor Constantine, was carefully cultivated by his descendants.

It is wrong to think of these kings simply as the product of royal

image makers and to doubt their beliefs.
Constantine II, one of Scotland's greatest
early medieval kings, retired from the
kingship after 40 turbulent years to become
abbot of the monastery at **St Andrews**. He
was not forced into retirement, and the
deep Christian convictions which led him
into religious life can be traced throughout
his career. Remembered as the king who
forged a new partnership with his Church,
and as a generous patron of monasteries
and befriender of holy men, he also allied
with the pagan Norse. Warlord and master
politician, he encapsulated in one man the
contradictions of piety and worldliness that
characterised the rulers of that age.

Constantine's successors maintained the
partnership between Church and Crown.
The flow of royal gifts, ostensibly a mark of
piety and devotion to God but probably
more an effort to win clerical support by
kings whose grip on the throne was
challenged, continued despite upheavals
within the dynasty. In the 11th century, for example, Macbeth sought
to establish his grasp on power by courting the Church. Generosity,
however, was tempered with practicality, for the Church was used in
return as a source of patronage. Necessity perhaps required Macbeth
to grant the abbacies of wealthy monasteries to lay nobles whose
loyalty he needed. Gifts of land and privileges were for him both
calculated bids for Church support and acts of piety. Even his
pilgrimage to Rome in 1050 carried as many political as religious
motives. Yet for all these centuries of donations and evidence for
contact with Rome, the Scottish Church in the 11th century was
falling out of step with the tide of reform which was sweeping
Europe.

Restenneth Priory, Forfar, Angus. Politics lay behind the foundation of the 8th-century church, dedicated to St Peter, which is believed to lie below the site of the 12th-century priory at Restenneth. Following the defeat of the Picts by the Northumbrians in 711, the Pictish king Nechtan abandoned his support for the Celtic clergy and adopted the Roman usages followed by his vanquishers. At his request, Northumbrian priests were sent to Pictland as architects to build a new church of stone (Shepherd).

REVIVAL, REFORMATION AND SPIRITUAL REVOLUTION

A key role in introducing the practices of the reinvigorated
Continental Church which emerged in the 11th century was held by
Margaret, second wife of Malcolm III. Of Anglo-Saxon royal blood,
she had been raised in recently converted Hungary with her exiled

family. Hungary had experienced the full vigour of the reformed Church, and Margaret had grown up in this atmosphere of new-found religious fervour pioneered by the spiritual shock troops of the reform movement, and the experience instilled in her a deep spirituality. While there was much in the Scottish Church that appealed to that spirituality, such as the tradition of holy men living

Scotland's royal saint. Reconstruction of St Margaret's shrine, Dunfermline Abbey, Fife. While she did not achieve single-handedly the overnight transformation of the Scottish Church, Margaret, second wife of Malcolm III, imbued her sons with a devotion to the Continental Church which was to lead to the complete reconstruction of the native system within half a century of her death (Historic Scotland).

a simple life as hermits, in its basic practices there was much that jarred her personal beliefs. With the support of King Malcolm, and assisted by three monks sent from Canterbury as the basis of a priory at **Dunfermline,** Margaret began in a small way to introduce the Scots to the reformed Roman Church.

These first steps almost failed in the upheavals which followed Malcolm and Margaret's deaths in 1093, but her influence on her sons ensured future success. In them she inspired outstanding spiritual zeal and devotion to the reformed ways, which they put into practice once they had established their hold on the kingdom. Thus the reigns of Edgar, Alexander I and, especially, David I saw a wave of monastic foundations and appointments of reformed clergy to bishoprics. This achievement can be dismissed cynically as the work of men seeking to use the new power of the Church to enhance personal reputations, but this fails to recognise that their actions were part of a movement whose consequences were as far-reaching as the 16th-century Protestant Reformation.

Margaret's sons believed firmly that the prayers of the new monastic orders spawned by the reform movement made them the perfect intercessors between God and mankind. At their supplication, divine mercy could be called down on the souls of the dead. The self-denying lifestyle of some of the monks was believed to make them spiritually purer and therefore closer to God. Their prayers were regarded as the most effective of all. Since the king of Scots wanted to have God on his side, it was these new orders who benefited most from royal patronage.

Scotland's royal monastic foundations c. AD 1080–1231.

Urquhart
Kinloss
Pluscarden

Restenneth
Coupar
Arbroath
Scone
Balmerino
Loch Leven
May Island
Dunfermline
Cambuskenneth
Inchcolm
Manuel
Holyrood
Coldingham
Newbattle
Kelso
Melrose
Jedburgh

Holmcultram

‡   Early Canmore Kings c. 1080 - 1124

‡   David I 1124-1153

‡   Malcolm IV, William and Alexander II

THE 'SAIR SANCT FOR THE CROUN' AND HIS LEGACY

The greatest contribution to the wave of reform was made by **David I**. His education at the English court had made him deeply conscious of the value of highly trained clerics to royal government, but exposed him also to the dynamism of the new ideals through contact with the expanding monastic orders. Indeed, his personal beliefs were such that he tried to meet one of the greatest holy men of his day, **St Bernard of Tiron**, founder of the Tironensian order.

David began to put his faith into practice when he was bequeathed southern Scotland by his elder brother, Edgar. He immediately appointed his chaplain, John, as reforming bishop of **Glasgow**, and followed this in 1113 with the foundation of an abbey at **Selkirk**, transplanted in 1128 to **Kelso.** David showed his admiration for St Bernard by colonising it with monks brought direct from Tiron as the first community of any reformed order anywhere in Britain.

In his lifetime David I gained a reputation for piety. It was a cultivated image which lifted his kingship onto a spiritual plain, while glossing over the less-than-saintly life of the king as warlord. It is seen strikingly in this 19th century facsimile of the portrayal of David on a charter to Kelso Abbey of his successor, Malcolm IV. David appears as Solomon, the perfect Biblical king, enthroned in majesty, with the long hair and beard of a patriarch. Such imagery became a powerful tool in the making of the dynasty.

David succeeded to the throne in 1124, and as king carried through the reforms which his parents and brothers had begun. Generosity to the Church was the hallmark of his reign and won him a reputation for piety. Indeed, so generous was he to the monasteries which he founded that James I caustically remarked that David had been 'ane sair sanct for the croun', plundering royal revenues to endow churches. James, though, was looking back from an age when the zeal of the reformers had withered, and viewed David's benevolence as a wasted investment. David, had been certain that he would receive value for money through the prayers and masses which the monks offered for the salvation of his family and people.

Malcolm IV, David's grandson, inherited the spirituality of his forbears, but his beliefs went further towards the perfect icon of Christ the King in the form of a vow of personal chastity. It was a decision, applauded by his clergy, which underscored the intensity of Malcolm's faith through placing of personal conviction before his duty to ensure the succession.

His reign coincided with the climax of the reforms which reshaped the Scottish Church. Under his successors the flow of gifts and the foundation of abbeys continued, but the pace slackened. Perceptions, too, were changing as men observed how wealth which pious benefactors had showered on the monasteries had blunted the traditions of austerity and piety. Simplicity and purity of lifestyle were still seen as indicators of spirituality, so men looked to newer, more austere orders, such as the Valliscaulians for whom Alexander II founded the last great royal monastery of that age in 1231 at **Pluscarden** in Moray. Already by that date new types of religious order were taking the place at the forefront of spirituality held previously by the monks.

CHANGING DIRECTIONS

The foundation of the **Dominican** and **Franciscan** orders of friars saw a fresh wave of intense spirituality sweep Europe. Their life of poverty and role as preachers won them quick popularity, for they filled a spiritual void left by disillusionment with the monastic orders. The simple requirements of the friars were attractive

Pluscarden Priory, Moray. Its foundation in 1231 by Alexander II, probably as a thanks offering for his final victory over his MacWilliam rivals, marked the culmination of over a century of royal patronage of the monastic orders (Shepherd).

to kings who wished to show devotion to the Church, but for whom foundation of an abbey had become unaffordable. Before the end of Alexander II's reign, friaries had been founded from Berwick to Inverness. This image of conventional piety is tempered by Alexander's clear understanding of the worldly benefits which it brought to his kingship. It was in his reign, for example, that the efforts to have Margaret canonised intensified, probably through recognition of the lustre which a saintly ancestor would cast on the monarchy. It also held a powerful political message, too, for in Margaret the Scots had their royal saint to match the English Edward the Confessor, with the added factor that her holy blood flowed in the veins of Scottish kings.

Despite such displays of continued devotion to God, whatever the underlying motive, attitudes towards the Church had changed markedly in the century after the death of David I. In particular, as the pioneering zeal of the monks faded, and a sense that the task of spiritual renewal was complete grew, the relationship between Crown and clergy changed. Whereas in the past the king had made sure that leading members of the reformed orders had been appointed to bishoprics, the wealth and power of high office in the Church came to be seen as fitting reward for dedicated service to the Crown. Clerks, whose continued loyalty to the Crown could be assumed, generally filled important vacancies. This was accompanied by a subtle change in what the king expected from the Church. Rather than purely spiritual rewards, the king looked increasingly for political support.

THE FIRST ESTATE

This attitude was reinforced in the 14th century, when the Church's place as the 'first estate', or represented group in parliament, confirmed the important place in secular politics which its landed wealth had established. The lavish gifts showered on the Church by Robert I were made partly in thanksgiving for God's support for his cause and in atonement for crimes committed on his path to the throne, but were largely rewards for the support given by the clergy in the struggle for independence. Gifts, however, could not guarantee enduring loyalty, so Robert continued to appoint royal servants to key positions in the Church, so providing a further prop for his new regime.

Under the Stewarts these trends accelerated as kings came to regard the Church as almost a department of government. Their concern for its well-being was matched by determination to capitalise on papal weakness. As a result, concessions were wrung from popes who needed support against their enemies. The Church, too, continued to be used as a means of enhancing royal reputations. James I, better remembered as the king who criticised David I's spending on the Church, cashed in on popular dissatisfaction by presenting himself as a concerned, reform-minded ruler. Although his parliaments legislated against corruption, and the king was preparing a reforming council when he was assassinated, James's actions were designed to enhance his prestige. His greatest act, the foundation of a priory at Perth in 1429, was designed to exalt the splendid new style of kingship which James was building in Scotland. For all his posturing, the decline of the Church continued unchecked.

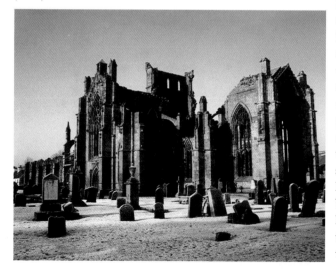

Melrose Abbey, Roxburghshire. Support for the Bruce cause in the Wars of Independence brought generous rewards for the Church from a grateful monarch. In his role as renewer of Scottish freedom and heir to Scotland's ancient kings, Robert acted as a benevolent patron. Melrose, a monastery connected intimately with the monarchy, enjoyed his sustained patronage, culminating in the grant of £2000 towards the costs of rebuilding the war-damaged abbey (Oram).

A DEN OF THIEVES

By the 15th century, displays of royal piety had become little more than exercises in public relations. Anti-clerical legislation, usually presented as reform, always won popular support, while new foundations and magnificent building projects served to emphasise personal devotion and added to the aura of majesty surrounding the kings. The Crown, however, continued the trend of using Church office as rewards for service, a process which accelerated after 1487 when James III extracted from the pope the right to make appointments to important benefices. While many capable men received appointments in this way, the system was open to abuse. Under **James IV**, such appointments allowed the king to bring the Church more closely under royal control. In 1497 he appointed

his younger brother, the **Duke of Ross**, as archbishop of St Andrews, placing a royal prince at the head of the Church. Following Ross's death in 1504, James appointed a 12-year-old royal bastard, **Alexander** and, since he was under age, kept control of the archbishopric in his hands. While James's motives were for the extension of royal power over the Church, he did take care to appoint suitable candidates, or, as in the case of Alexander, to have them educated for their office.

William Elphinstone, Bishop of Aberdeen (1483–1514); bronze memorial (1911, H Wilson) King's College, Old Aberdeen. Perhaps the most capable of the civil-servant bishops of the later Middle Ages, he was able to serve both his royal masters as chancellor (until 1488) and a judge, and to actively fulfil his duties as a diocesan pastor. A conscientious priest, he introduced new service and devotional books to encourage popular devotions; his greatest monument is the university which he founded at Aberdeen (Shepherd).

PILGRIMS OR PLAY–ACTORS

Counterbalancing Crown interference in Church affairs was the personal piety of the king. Displays of faith, such as James III's magnificent altarpiece for **Trinity College** in Edinburgh, could be cynically stage-managed occasions, but were also part of a shift towards a fashion for public demonstrations of devotion. The most striking manifestation of this was pilgrimage. The tradition of spiritual journeys to the tombs of saints was embedded in popular Christianity. In Scotland a fashion for royal pilgrimage was begun by Robert I in the 14th century, who in his latter years journeyed to **Whithorn** in search of a cure for a debilitating skin disease. His son, David II, continued the practice, being cured at **St Monan's** shrine

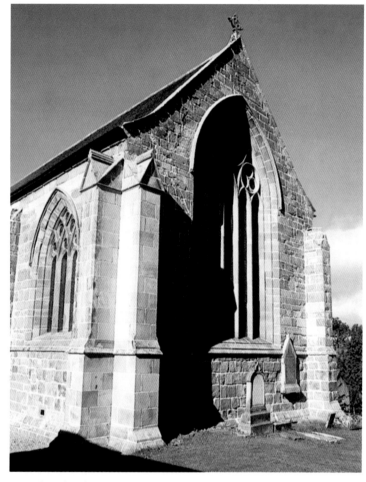

St Duthac's Kirk, Tain, Ross-shire. Royal veneration of this obscure northern saint saw James IV make annual pilgrimages to his shrine. James was ostentatious in his devotion to Duthac, commissioning new reliquaries to contain the saint's remains and making generous gifts of alms to the church, but more was spent on the king's personal appearance for these highly public occasions (Oram).

in Fife of a head wound received in 1346. In thanksgiving he founded a new church.

It was James IV, however, who made pilgrimage an art form. The beliefs which drove him to travel annually to Whithorn and **Tain** were hedged with practical objectives. His pilgrimages formed part of an upsurge in popular devotion, which saw the foundation of new chaplainries, the creation of new collegiate churches, and revival of interest in the friaries. They also served worldly ends. James's pilgrimages took him into remote corners of Scotland and displayed the majesty of the Crown in areas far removed from the centres of power. They were often well planned and highly theatrical, with the king spending more on clothing for the occasion than on offerings made at the shrine, but some were spontaneous, with James travelling with the minimum of show.

St Andrews Cathedral, Fife. Although the Crown presented itself as protector and reformer of the Scottish Church, heavy taxation and the plundering of its resources to provide royal patronage demoralised the senior clergy at the time when the Protestant challenge was first emerging. The close association of the archbishop of St Andrews with unpopular pro-French policies further undermined support for an already beleaguered institution (Oram).

THE TURN OF THE WHEEL

The upsurge in spirituality evident under James IV represented a last flourishing of the medieval Church on the eve of the Reformation. **James V** threatened reform as a lever to extract concessions from the papacy, and so tightened his grip on the Church. Like his father, he was concerned for the spiritual welfare of his kingdom and encouraged the process of internal reform within the monastic orders, but his piety was offset by pragmatism, for religion had become a matter of politics. The Church offered James a convenient source of revenue, but heavy taxes weakened it at a time when it needed to respond to the challenges of Protestantism. Furthermore, his control of appointments became an exercise in royal patronage, with rich monasteries becoming prized gifts for loyal servants, or endowments for the king's bastard sons. For James, Reformation had little to offer in the way of tangible gains, and his faith was not sufficiently strong to push him along that road. By the same token his personal convictions were not strong enough to bring him to carry through a genuine reform of the existing structure. In him, the pious efforts of 400 years of Scottish kings and the role of the Crown as a fount of inspiration in the religious life of the kingdom ended. When Reformation came, it was carried through against the wishes of the Crown, and although **James VI** was eventually to establish a close relationship with the reformed Kirk, for him and his descendants it was a relationship based entirely on politics rather than piety.

CHAPTER 6

ROYAL
TRAVELLERS

I n this chapter we look at the most basic fact of life for any Scottish monarch who sought effectively to rule the kingdom: travel.

Travelling was more of a fact of life to the royalty of medieval Scotland than it is to our present-day rulers, yet many of the basic reasons which required our early kings to traverse the kindom hold true for modern government. There is a need to be seen in areas that may feel neglected or vulnerable, be it as the result of some natural catastrophe or accident, or where political concerns show votes to be fragile. Above all it is a means of familiarising the populations of districts remote from the political hub with the living symbols of national unity.

Television and other media now mean that touring is less crucial to government, but for the early rulers without these benefits regular travelling was a vital tool for binding the kingdom together. Kings travelled to allow their people to see them, for, other than a tiny stereotyped image stamped on a coin, few folk in the nation's peripheries would have known who their ruler was, let alone what he or she looked like. Like modern fact-finding missions this was a two-way process, for travel allowed the monarch to familiarise himself with his people and the problems of government in areas remote from his main centres of power. In the formative years of the kingdom in the 12th and 13th centuries, royal power expanded through the establishment of colonial aristocracies in outlying regions, begun by the king and shaped under his personal direction.

OPPOSITE: *Hermitage Castle, Roxburghshire. Queen Mary's cross-country ride to Hermitage to visit the wounded Earl of Bothwell in October 1566 has been portrayed as the mad expedition of a love-sick woman, but was well within the capabilities of a ruler born to govern from the saddle (Oram).*

For Scotland's medieval monarchs, it was essential to travel widely round the kingdom to impose their will in the localities. This 19th-century depiction of Queen Victoria shows the continuation of the horse-riding monarch.

The effort of travel

Until 1561, when Mary imported the first coach from France, all royal expeditions were undertaken on horseback. Although, in common with all nobles, Scotland's medieval rulers were raised to a life in the saddle, their role involved long and arduous expeditions through a land which lacked good roads. The physical demands of such journeys for a fit and experienced rider should not, perhaps, be overstated – for example, Mary's infamous ride from Jedburgh to Hermitage in 1566, noted on p.83. However, for elderly men, such as William the Lion or Robert II, the stress of government from horseback took a heavy toll upon their health.

There were also down-to-earth considerations which required the king to travel. Firstly, the king in his court represented the supreme source of justice in the realm, and was expected to visit the main regional centres on a regular basis to dispense the law. Failure to provide 'good justice' was an accusation levelled against later medieval kings who preferred to base themselves on Edinburgh and Stirling. Secondly, in the earlier Middle Ages, the Crown received much revenue in kind, mainly agricultural produce, and this accumulated at administrative centres. Added to this were renders from royal estates, together representing a mass of foodstuffs. In an age when it was difficult and costly to transport supplies in bulk, or where access to a market with sufficient demand for such quantities was limited, it was easier for king and household to travel to the provinces and consume the produce on the spot. In the later Middle Ages the problem was frequently reversed, with the presence of the king and court in the provincial centres being undesirable locally. Large households placed a major strain on the ability of local markets to satisfy demand for even basic foodstuffs, often resulting in shortages or the artificial inflation of prices by merchants determined to cash in on the royal presence. Finally, the primitive sanitary arrangements at the royal residences meant that prolonged occupation made them unsavoury places to linger. The court needed to move frequently to allow the cleansing and airing of the palaces.

In an age where government revolved around the king and his followers, travel was essential for the exercise of government. From the 12th century, when the monarchy began to produce large quantities of parchment records, we can see this restless style of kingship in action. While earlier kings were undoubtedly as mobile, it is with David I that we begin to see a monarchy that was becoming truly national in the way in which it reached out to the remoter regions of the kingdom. In his 29-year reign, David's travels carried him from **Inverness** to **Carlisle** – and beyond – while his grandson, William the Lion, took the royal presence into Galloway and Caithness. The mobility of 12th-century kings, moreover, is underscored by the spread of royal castles with hunting preserves in their neighbourhood (see Chapter 7). These were residences which the kings used when travelling around the kingdom to dispense justice and supervise the establishment of local administrations.

GETTING THE SHOW ON THE ROAD

Then, as now, royal progresses were no simple exercise. In place of press corps, secretaries, bodyguards and communications teams, there

George, 5th Lord Seton, Master of the Household to Mary Queen of Scots. Portrait attributed to Adrian Vanson, in the Scottish National Portrait Gallery, Edinburgh (reproduced by kind permission of The Scottish National Portrait Gallery).

was the household and its various departments to be transported, together with the king himself and his officers and advisors. The lists of dignitaries attached as witnesses to charters granted by the king whilst on his travels reveals how substantial this mobile retinue could be, and when some of the greater nobles accompanied the king, their following considerably added to the total. An efficient secretariat ensured that the household was well-supplied, and masterminded the unceasing task of transporting the apparatus which enabled its smooth running around the kingdom.

Accommodation for the mobile household was one of the headaches facing the clerks who managed its routine. In the 12th and 13th centuries, the less elaborate household could be fitted into the royal castles spread around the country, while the greater nobles who joined the royal retinue often possessed properties in the burghs which lay alongside the castles. In the later Middle Ages, the main household could be accommodated with ease in the larger palaces, with room for important individuals only becoming a problem during the great occasions of state, but expeditions away from the principal centres caused serious difficulties. Hospitality was expected of monasteries and the castles of the greater nobles in districts where there was no royal residence, but where these were lacking desperate measures were called for. In 1563, for example, on Mary's progress through Galloway, the queen imposed herself on several lesser lairds. At tiny Corra Castle, while Mary could expect the laird to surrender the comforts of his own chamber to her, the gentlemen who accompanied her had to bed down in the cramped hall or in the out-buildings and byres. Such were the hazards of royal travel.

The mobile household remained a major aspect of royal life down to the end of the 14th century. Robert II was the last king until James IV to travel regularly and extensively throughout his kingdom, and increasingly in the 15th century Scotland's rulers moved within a triangle defined by **Edinburgh**, **Stirling** and **Perth**, with occasional forays to outlying locations. A variety of factors contributed to this situation. In the first place, the Wars of Independence had seen the destruction of many royal castles, such as Aberdeen, Dundee and Perth, and other residences, such as Roxburgh and Jedburgh, remained in English hands into the 15th century. The increasing delegation of power in the provinces, moreover, required kings to travel less to dispense justice. It was also impractical for the administrative arm of the household to move regularly, especially as it became more sophisticated and relied less on the personal involvement of the king. Specialist departments, such as the chancellor's office, had become too cumbersome to transport easily, and by the 15th century had put down roots in Edinburgh. Mobility may have ceased to be part of the function of government, but it remained a vital aspect of kingship.

'HOME IS WHERE I LOVE THE BEST': THE DANGERS OF IMMOBILITY

Amongst the principal factors involved in the erosion of royal power after 1390 was the **internal exile** of the king, Robert III, to his personal estates in the west. Robert had been excluded from power by his younger brother, and rarely stirred from his castles of Rothesay and Dundonald other than for ceremonial appearances. Much royal power in the provinces had already been delegated to members of the Stewart family or of the higher nobility, but Robert's inability to travel saw them establish themselves as the visible symbols of authority within their spheres of influence: men looked to them rather than to the remote figure of the king for lordship and protection. The captivity of James I led to an entrenchment of this position, and even the Duke of Albany, governor in the captive king's name, rarely travelled outwith the area where his faction was strongest. By the time of James's release, some areas of the kingdom had not seen the person of the king for nearly 40 years.

Dundonald Castle, Ayrshire: a reconstruction of the Great Hall. Excluded from an active role in the government of the kingdom, Robert III held court in this hill-top fortress as king of little more than his personal lands in the west of Scotland, in reality in immobile exile in his own realm (Historic Scotland).

For James I and James II, the need to re-establish royal power after periods of erosion, or to settle political disturbances in remote parts of the realm, saw a return to the tradition of **royal progresses** and the holding of parliaments and courts away from the centres of government. Challenges in the north took James I to Aberdeen, Inverness and Dingwall, and to Dunstaffnage in Argyll, while James II's struggle with the Douglases took him as far as Wigtown in Galloway. For the most part, however, these were military expeditions rather than leisurely tours, and were undertaken with the aim of so cowing these troublesome zones as to ensure that the king could sit in Edinburgh or Stirling secure in the knowledge that his will went unchallenged. Under James III, the tendency for the court to stir rarely beyond Edinburgh provoked crisis: centralisation of power was seen as neglect of the needs of the country in general. In particular James's failure to travel to dispense justice was regarded as symbolic of widespread lack of good government. It was one mistake which his son was not to repeat, for James IV reverted to the traditional royal routine of mobility.

TRANSPORTS OF DELIGHT

It is from the reign of James IV that a clearer picture emerges of the **logistical problem** of transporting the household round even its reduced circuit of the palaces at Edinburgh, Linlithgow, Stirling and Falkland. Administrative records, such as the Chamberlain Rolls, show that when the king was absent the palaces were run on a care-and-maintenance basis. The buildings were furnished at a rudimentary level, containing only essential equipment and such materials as would allow an unexpected visit by the king to be accommodated, as happened when he decided to escape the routine of government for a few days hunting. The bulk of the staff and royal furnishings and equipment were transported from place to place as the king moved around, packed into a train of wagons hired or requisitioned from private carriers. All the furnishings which added lustre to the court of the later Stewarts was transported with the household.

The scale of James's **mobile household** increased substantially after his marriage to Margaret Tudor. The queen had her own separate establishment to transport, including a train of ladies-in-waiting with their beds and baggage, and a wardrobe that required several wagons in its own right. It is clear from the barbed comments in the records that the veterans of James's bachelor establishment found the ladies an encumbrance, slowing down the progress of the retinue and disturbing their routine with complaints about management of the operation or suitability of accommodation. There is obvious relief evident when the king and queen travelled separately, and Margaret often chose to stay in the properties assigned to her as part of her marriage portion while James travelled around

Linlithgow Palace, West Lothian: reconstruction of the Court Kitchen and GreatHall in the time of James IV (Historic Scotland). For his Easter and Christmas courts at Linlithgow, James carried everything from his chairs of state to the more basic domestic paraphernalia. His more workaday visits to the palaces away from Edinburgh did cause problems. When foreign ambassadors arrived unexpectedly at Linlithgow during one of the king's brief visits, servants had to hurry back to Edinburgh to bring fine wall-hangings and the best altar vessels for the chapel to allow the king to put on a good show.

on his official duties. James himself clearly felt impeded by slow-moving baggage trains, and often used flittings between palaces as an excuse to escape for a few days' hunting in the Highlands.

Of course, James and Margaret did not drag the full household with them on every journey. Both travelled with much-reduced trains on their pilgrimages to Whithorn and Tain, but these were still regal progresses designed to impress their subjects as much as they were pious journeys. James, however, often travelled faster and lighter. Tradition records how, on whim, with only a small escort he rode from Stirling to Elgin by way of Perth and Aberdeen in a single day, and on to Tain the following morning. Such journeys ensured that James knew the kingdom better than any of his predecessors, but ensured too that he was known more intimately by his people than any previous ruler. Indeed, James used his travels to win easy popularity with his subjects, for his

financial accounts show how every journey saw the continual distribution of largesse – gifts of money – to the folk, great and small, whom he encountered along the way. The measure of James's success can be seen in the internal peace and stability of most of the kingdom during his reign, and the sense of the passing of a second golden age which followed his death at Flodden.

Moves between palaces was no simple exercise for the medieval court. Royal residences were normally furnished at only a basic level, and all the more sophisticated trappings of monarchy had to be packed and transported on lumbering wagons whenever the court moved on. Image showing ladies in a carriage drawn from the Luttrell Psalter (Shepherd).

DAUNTING JOURNEYS

In the changed political climate of the 16th century, progresses assumed greater importance than simple public relations exercises. While James V continued his father's policy of reaching into the peripheries of his realm, his journeys increasingly took on the character of **punitive raids** designed to daunt troublesome regions. James sought to enforce the submissiveness of outlying

The Sound of Mull, Argyll. For James IV and James V, determination to tighten the grip of royal government on their realm meant the mounting of military expeditions into even the remote and stormy waters of the Hebrides, far from the comforts of court (Oram).

regions, but used terror rather than the courting of popularity to achieve his ends. His expedition into the Borders in 1529–30 was a visitation of royal justice on a region where reiving and banditry was endemic, but acts of calculated terror, including the summary execution of brigands, while successful in the short term, left a legacy of bitterness. It took many years of judicial expeditions into the Borders by Mary and James VI to re-establish the royal grip in that unruly zone. Displays of military might and the magnificence of his kingship had similar underlying objectives. James V's most ambitious venture came in 1540 when, with 12 ships, he became the first Scottish monarch to sail round his country from east to west. The cruise was a glittering affair designed to overawe opposition to the royal will in Orkney and the Hebrides, but the heavily-armed vessels had teeth which James was prepared to use if need be.

For James V's daughter, Mary, travel fulfilled many objectives. Having left Scotland in 1548, she had little knowledge of the kingdom to which she returned in 1561, nor did Mary's subjects have much knowledge of her. It was also vital that she reassert royal power after 18 years of regency government and bitter civil war. As a consequence, Mary's first foray from Edinburgh in September 1561 took the form of a progress through the heart of her kingdom, introducing her to her main palaces and population centres in a broad sweep through Lothian to Stirling, on to Perth and Dundee, returning to Holyroodhouse via St Andrews and Falkland. While this first expedition was designed for its spectacle, her second journey, which took her into the north of Scotland, had political motives behind it. At once satisfying Mary's adventurous spirit, the objective of the long journey to Inverness via Aberdeen was to assess the reliability of the Earl of Huntly, the most powerful nobleman in the north. The queen's retinue, however, formed a core

One of Mary Queen of Scots' journeys in her Progress around the realm.

around which to build an army when the progress turned into a military campaign which culminated in Huntly's defeat and death.

THE END OF THE ROAD

Mary's reign saw the last large-scale royal expeditions around the kingdom until the 19th century. While the same complex interplay of political necessity and image building which underpinned Mary's travels is evident in her son's progresses, James VI, before his departure for London in 1603, rarely travelled beyond the secure heart of his realm. His expeditions to the Borders combined his grandfather's ruthless reimposition of the royal will with the military overawing of opposition pursued in the Isles in 1540 or against Huntly in 1562, but James in the late 1590s was still accused of laziness and of entrusting to deputies the task of carrying the royal writ into outlying regions rather than undertaking the responsibility in person. All such personal expeditions by Scotland's rulers ended abruptly in 1603, terminating a practice which had been a most effective tool in the task of welding together the kingdom.

With the exception of his return visit to Scotland in 1617, and his son's coronation visit in 1633, James VI's triumphant progress from Edinburgh to Berwick and entry into his new realm marked the last formal royal journey through Scotland until George IV visited Edinburgh in 1822. Rather than political necessity, that trip was sparked more by royal curiosity to visit a part of the kingdom which the writings of Sir Walter Scott had rehabilitated as a romantic land of wild and rugged grandeur peopled by the descendants of the heroic figures who stalked his Waverley novels. Standing armies and parliamentary patronage had replaced most of the reasons which had obliged George's medieval ancestors to travel, reducing this first royal visit since the 17th century to the equivalent of a tourist jaunt. The precedent established in 1822 took firm root, and once Victoria had given the seal of approval to all things Scottish, an annual visit and residence in Scotland became fixed events in the royal calendar. These new royal travels in Scotland, however, were more than simple holiday trips, for they formed a central part in the integration of the Scots into the wider British monarchy and its 19th-century empire. Like James IV before them, Victoria and her descendants used their travels through the kingdom to fix themselves at the heart of the social life of the land.

CHAPTER 7

THE SPORT OF KINGS

ROYALTY AT LEISURE

We have looked so far at the formal, public face of Scotland's royalty, at the structures and methods of government which supported it and in particular the relationship of the Church which lay at the heart of much royal image building.

A ROYAL PASSION FOR THE CHASE

In this last chapter we turn our attention to another facet of the public image of royalty, but one which was considerably less formal – their leisure pursuits. Photographs of Edward VII or George V on the grouse moors, or of the present Queen Mother fishing for salmon, present them as active and vigorous, and, incidentally, show them in relaxation as inheritors of activities strongly associated with past rulers, in particular that most aristocratic of pursuits, hunting. Royal passion for stalking or the chase in the 19th century was the rediscovery of pursuits enjoyed by their medieval ancestors. From almost as soon as we have documentary records of the new style of kingship created by the sons of Malcolm III and Margaret in the early 12th century we have evidence for their passionate involvement in **hunting** and **hawking.**

However, they were not the first of Scotland's kings for whom the hunt was the favourite leisure-time activity: it was a royal and aristocratic accomplishment centuries before they turned it into an art form. Embedded in the semi-legendary tales of early Celtic kings are stories of the hunt and instances of epic heroism which pitched kings and warriors against mystical beasts. Hunting scenes are fossilised in carvings on **Pictish symbol stones**, depicting great men and ladies on horseback, accompanied by runners, hounds and trumpeters in pursuit of stags. All the action and energy of springing hounds and fleeing deer is caught by the sculptors, but so too is the

OPPOSITE: *One of royalty's main pursuits: portrait of James VI, seen here as a young boy with his hawk, by Arnold Bronckorst (reproduced by kind permission of The Scottish National Portrait Gallery).*

Hunt scene of the 9th century AD on the Aberlemno Roadside Pictish cross slab. From earliest times, hunting with hawks and hounds has been regarded as one of the traditional accomplishments of nobility and royalty. Throughout their recorded history, the chase was a consuming passion of Scottish monarchs, male and female alike (Historic Scotland).

nobility of the hunters. This is the sport of kings, not of peasants.

The status of hunting, particularly of deer, and of hawking as the exclusive preserve of the king and favoured nobles was established in the early 12th century in Scotland. Hunting rights were amongst the most jealously guarded privileges of the Norman nobles who conquered England in the 11th century, and royal devotees went to extraordinary lengths to safeguard both hunting land and game. Large tracts of the English countryside were designated hunting forest and placed under harsh forest laws. Severe restrictions were imposed on the way of life of folk who lived within an afforested area and savage penalties inflicted on those who damaged the quality of the hunting by clearing land for cultivation or by erecting barriers, or who dared poach deer. This view of hunting was introduced to Scotland by kings educated in Norman ways, and its status as the exclusive right of the Crown, bestowed as a gift on the most privileged amongst the nobility, was enshrined in law.

As in England, tracts of woodland and moor were designated **hunting forest**. Although there were legal restrictions placed on the inhabitants of these areas, there were none of the harsh forest laws of England. Nevertheless, hunting grounds and hunting rights were prized possessions, defended with energy, and there are instances of long-running court cases concerning infringements of

Map of royal hunting forests.

restrictions, especially where the felling of trees or grazing threatened the habitat of the quarry.

The scale of royal forests and their spread across the country was staggering. David I and Malcolm IV had their favourite hunting-lands mainly in the Borders: the forests of **Ettrick** or **Selkirk** and the smaller forest of **Jedburgh**. In Lothian, David had the **King's Park** around

Arthur's Seat close to his castle at Edinburgh: while hunting there in 1128 David was gored by a stag and narrowly escaped death, an event which formed the core of the foundation legend of Holyrood Abbey. David also had forests further to the north, such as **Longmorn** and **Darnaway** in Moray, established soon after the conquest of the region in the 1130s, for use when he visited his castles at Elgin and Forres. The most favoured late 12th- and 13th-century forests, however, fringed the mountainous country between Strathmore and the River Dee. Here were the forests of **Birse** and **Cowie**, and the most important of the early northern deer parks, **Kincardine**. It is possible that Kincardine was a royal hunting ground in the 10th century: local tradition, first recorded in the 14th century, claimed that it was while on a hunting trip near here that Kenneth II was murdered in 995. It was a favoured hunting seat in the reigns of William the Lion and his son, Alexander II, used as a resting place on their regular journeys to the north while on campaign against rebels in Moray and Ross.

In the wars which ravaged Scotland between 1296 and 1314, and from 1332 until 1357, kings had little time to spend in hunting. Many hunting preserves fell into disuse and while Robert I ordered the repair of some parks, as at the Forest of **Drum** in Aberdeenshire, others were never reinstated. Some forests popular with 13th-century kings lay in the zones exposed to English raids, or occupied by English garrisons – for example, Jedburgh was held by the English until 1410 – so northern forests enjoyed a new popularity.

Under the Stewarts hunting enjoyed a revival. The founder of the dynasty, Robert II, was a passionate hunter and in his regular tours around his kingdom made frequent use of his forests and parks. He conducted business of state while living at his hunting-lodges, as

The Kincardine royal hunting grounds

At Kincardine it is possible to see what one of these hunting grounds was like. To the north of the castle the ground rises rapidly into the Mounth, a high table-land scarred by deep watercourses and with woodland clinging to the lower slopes. The moors offered good sport, but, to guarantee a bag, an area of ground was emparked – enclosed by a bank and ditch and crowned with a timber palisade – and stocked with deer (Shepherd).

Hallforest Castle, Kintore, Aberdeenshire. English occupation of much of southern Scotland during the Wars of Independence saw the ancient royal hunting lands in northern Scotland find renewed favour with Robert I and his successors. Amongst the most important of these was the Forest of Kintore where, soon after 1309, Sir Robert Keith built the gaunt tower which served as a royal hunting-lodge for Robert I and David II (Oram).

charters issued by him at recognised hunting centres such as Kindrochit (where he built a new castle), Glen Finglas, Strath Braan, Glen Almond, Glen Shee, Glen Prosen and Badenoch show. For him, though, hunting was more than simple recreation. Hunting parties allowed him to gather together members of his family, especially his sons into whose hands he had placed so much power within the kingdom, or to meet nobles informally. His passion for the hunt also had a place in royal image building. Robert, before he became king, had established ties with the Gaelic lords of the Highlands and Islands, and in many ways his family had become part of this Celtic aristocracy. In Gaelic noble society prowess in the hunt was an accomplishment praised and commemorated by bards, and Robert used his skills in the field to gain respect, and political support, from the Highland chiefs.

The reign of every Stewart from Robert II onwards saw maintenance of, or extensions to, royal hunting grounds. The main acquisition was Falkland in Fife, seized by the Crown on the execution of Walter Stewart, Earl of Atholl, for involvement in the assassination of his nephew, James I. It was the murdered king's son and successor, James II, who started to convert the fortress into what became the finest of the Stewarts' hunting lodges, **Falkland Palace**. Every ruler from James II to James VI used or extended the palace, transforming it into the Renaissance building which still dominants the tiny burgh which grew up at its gate.

Of all the later Stewart kings it was James IV who pursued hunting

Falkland Palace, Fife. The most magnificent of the Stewarts' hunting-lodges, the palace evolved as a summer residence for the Scottish kings from the mid 15th-century. It was the base for hunting expeditions into the moorland of the Lomond Hills and in the carefully husbanded oakwoods within its park enclosure (Oram).

with a passion close to that of his ancestor, Robert II. Like Robert, he used hunting trips to meet his nobility outwith the formality of court, and to visit parts of his realm where his predecessors had rarely travelled: **Glenartney**, **Glenfinglas** and **Darnaway** figured regularly on his itinerary. Planned hunts from **Edinburgh**, **Linlithgow** and **Stirling** regularly broke the routine of government, with instructions sent ahead of the travelling court to prohibit hunting to assure the king of a good bag. James spent lavishly on his sport: the remodelling of Falkland; new lodges at **Glenfinglas**; repairs to boundaries neglected during his father's reign; fine hounds and falcons obtained at great expense; captive herds transported from park to park to 'stock up' for a royal visit. But such expense was justified, for hunting was more than a pastime for James. It was an essential tool of monarchy, an accomplishment which cast as much lustre on the Crown as did military prowess or personal piety.

So central was hunting to royal life that even during the troubled 16th century efforts were made to maintain forests. In the 1550s, for example, the wood of Falkland, described as full of old and decayed trees, was felled and replanted to encourage game to settle and improve the hunting. Mary, raised at the French court where the hunt was viewed as one of the most important social functions of kingship, made a rare intervention in the business of her Privy Council to complain that acts prohibiting the shooting of deer were being ignored so that she and Darnley had 'na pastyme' at the chase. Hunting, too, formed an important element in the education of

James VI, and he was later accused of neglecting government to indulge his love. James's departure south, however, marked the end of royal hunting in Scotland for two and a half centuries, although at first the forests were maintained in expectation of royal visits. The crises of Charles I's reign led to the neglect and decline of the forests, reaching a symbolic nadir with Cromwell's conquest of Scotland in 1651. Having crushed support for the exiled Charles II, the last Stewart occupant of Falkland, in 1652 his administration began the systematic felling of the oakwoods to provide timber for a fortress at Perth, and in 1654 the palace itself was left in ruins: Falkland's destruction seemed to symbolise the fall of the Crown.

MORE TRIVIAL PURSUITS

Few other pursuits occupied Scotland's rulers with the same intensity as hunting, but it was not their sole leisure activity. In his eulogy for the murdered James I, the chronicler Walter Bower recorded that the king had excelled at **archery**, **jousting**, the **sling**, **hammer throwing**, **running**, **riding** and **wrestling**, skills which showed the physical prowess of the monarch in the best light. His great-grandson, James IV, enjoyed a similar reputation, and during his reign formal bow-butts for archery practice were laid out at Linlithgow and expensive specialist armour and equipment for use in the tiltyard at Edinburgh imported from the Continent.

REAL TENNIS

Another sport enjoyed at the Scottish court was **real tennis**. It is first mentioned in the reign of James I, whose interest in tennis contributed to his death in 1437: his assassins trapped him in a sewer whose end he had blocked after he had lost several balls in its depths. The game became more fashionable in the 16th century, and courts, or 'catchpules', were built at the royal palaces for James V. In Mary's reign there were courts at Holyrood and Linlithgow, but only that built at Falkland in 1539 for her father survives. It was an energetic sport, favoured by younger members of the household, and permitting the ruler to demonstrate skill and fitness. Royal records show that James V was a keen player, giving cash gifts to courtiers, visiting noblemen and household servants with whom he played, or betting on the outcome of matches between others. Tennis was one pursuit to which Mary's feckless husband, Lord Darnley, turned to vent his frustrations at his exclusion from a voice in government, but unpaid debts for supply of tennis balls suggest that his interest may have been fleeting. The game was more popular with their son, James

Real Tennis Court, Falkland Palace, Fife. The court or 'catchpule' at Falkland is the only survivor in Scotland of those built at every royal palace as part of the late medieval passion for tennis. The strenuous game was more than a simple recreation, instead forming part of courtly ritual through which the ruler could demonstrate manly skill, energy and athleticism (Shepherd).

VI, and his family, and it was Charles I who had the Falkland court repaved in 1628. As with the royal forest, however, the fall of the dynasty in the 1650s brought an end to its popularity and the courts fell into disuse. That at Holyrood survived until after 1714, when it was used as the venue for a play, but only that at Falkland remained to be restored in the 19th century.

INDOOR PASTIMES

Outdoor pursuits were not the only diversions for Scotland's rulers. Alongside his athletic skills, Bower claimed that James I was an accomplished **singer**, and played well on the **fiddle**, **psaltery**, **organ**, **flute**, **harp**, **trumpet** and **pipe**. James also turned his hand to **sketching** and **painting**, to **writing** and, above all, to **poetry**. It is easy to dismiss Bower's words as a recital of the stock imagery used to create an icon of the perfect king, presenting him as a paragon of royal virtues as a ruler and an inspirational personality, physically active, cultured and well educated, but his claims are supported by other evidence. His poem, 'The Kingis Quair', composed towards the end of his captivity in England, is a complex allegory on love and imprisonment built around the circumstances of his first encounter with his future wife, Joan Beaufort. It reveals depths of culture and sophistication in a man known mainly for his ruthless exercise of power. In it we can trace the influences of the poets Chaucer and

Gower, and the philosophical writings of Boethius can be seen in the king's musings on free will, pointing to the direction of James's interests during his 18-year captivity in England. Poetry and music remained dear to James, and he spent the evening of his murder playing the harp, singing and reading French romances in the company of Queen Joan.

The accounts of James's murder in 1437 reveal the king in his private moments, relaxing with his wife in a scene of domestic informality. No such pictures come down to us of his successors, but the household records of later Stewarts are rich in detail of informal aspects of their life. These draw colourful images of the kings and queens relaxing amongst their courtiers and servants, and of the entertainments and diversions which lightened the burden of government. Here is James IV enjoying the music of Highland harpers, giving gifts to the maidens of Linlithgow who sang

Indoor pursuits. A reconstruction of one of the entertainments for the royal court: bear-baiting in the hall at Dundonald Castle, Ayrshire (Historic Scotland).

Reconstruction of minstrels performing in the Great hall of Linlithgow Palace. Alongside the strenuous pursuits of hunting or tennis, Scotland's rulers enjoyed quieter moments of leisure at the heart of their family; music was then as now a major source of relaxation (Historic Scotland).

madrigals on Christmas morning, watching **tumblers** and **acrobats**, or laughing at his 'fool's' antics. He is there, too, borrowing money from courtiers and servants to **gamble** at cards and dice, sitting up until the early

morning playing his laundress – a notable card-sharp – and losing, then ordering his chamberlain to settle his debts from the privy purse. Such human traits bring James closer to us, adding flesh and personality to the one-dimensional figure who haunts our history books. It is a remarkably human picture of a king at ease with his people – a fitting image with which to end this review of Scotland's royalty and realm.

From the strongholds of the early centuries AD, seen reconstructed here, to the grand palaces of the 17th century, feasting and relaxation with families and courtiers would have provided a mainstay of leisure in the turbulent lives of Scotland's kings and queens.

GLOSSARY

Alba: early name used for the realm of Scotland in the 9th century AD

Burgess: originally any inhabitant of a *burgh* who held a piece of land there from the Crown or other superior lord, later restricted mainly to members of the merchant class and to the principal craftsmen

Burgh: privileged trading community (first recorded in Scotland in the early 12th century) which received charters from the Crown conferring extensive economic rights and jurisdictional liberties

Chamberlain: from the 12th century onwards the Crown's principal financial officer whose duties included supervision of the affairs of the burghs, which he visited on *ayre* (i.e. by circuit court)

Chancellor: chief legal officer of the Crown, first mentioned in the early 12th century, keeper of the *Great Seal* and overseer of the chancery, or royal writing office

Clarsach: ancient Highland style of harp

Collegiate Church: type of church deriving its name from the body of clergy – or 'college' – which served it, rendering complex services, with elaborate ritual and choral music

Comptroller: the 'roller of accounts', who, from the middle of the 15th century, shared financial administration with the *Treasurer*

Constable: officer responsible originally for securing the peace of the king's court and for organisation of the royal army

Dapifer: office of cup-bearer to the kings of Scots

Great Seal: principal royal seal, used to authenticate Crown charters and letters patent

Justiciar: from the 12th century, the king's chief jurisdictional deputy, whose duties included supervising the work of sheriffs and hearing law suits involving *Pleas of the Crown* or appeals from lesser courts

Minority: period of reign of a monarch acceding to throne whilst still a child until deemed to have gained majority (most usually between 18 and 21 years) to rule in own right

Mormaor: ruler of one of the great provinces of early Scotland before the 12th century, when the title was anglicised to 'earl'

Pleas of the Crown: cases involving certain crimes specifically reserved for trial in a royal court, by the 12th century restricted to arson, murder, rape and robbery, in addition to treason

Privy Council: select council, composed of the Crown's principal officers and advisers, which came into being in the early 16th century

Sheriff: general executive officer of the Crown in the localities, with administrative, financial and judicial functions

Steward: officer responsible for supervision and administration of the household; held from the 12th century by the fitz Alan family, ancestors of the Stewarts, who took their name from the office

Thane: originally a non-hereditary title applied to the administrator of an estate, but coming eventually to be a hereditary title of elevated social status

Treasurer: from the 15th century, chief officer sharing responsibility with the *Comptroller* for the royal finances

Vassal: holder of land directly from the king on conditions of homage and allegiance

INDEX

FURTHER READING

Such a wealth of literature exists on the subject of Scotland's kings and queens that it would be impossible to list it in full here. The following are consequently just some suggestions for further study; each will contain bibliographies to take the reader on to wider voyages of discovery.

GENERAL

Duncan, A A M, *Scotland: the Making of the Kingdom* (Edinburgh, 1978).

Lynch, M, *Scotland: a New History* (London, 1992).

Smyth, A P, *Warlords and Holy Men: Scotland AD 80 to 1000* (London, 1984).

INDIVIDUAL

Barrow, G W S, *Robert Bruce and the Community of the Realm of Scotland*, 3rd edn (Edinburgh, 1988).

Boardman, S I, *The Early Stewart Kings: Robert II and Robert III, 1371–1406* (East Linton, 1996).

Brown, M, *James I* (Edinburgh, 1994).

Fraser, A, *Mary Queen of Scots* (London, 1969).

Macdougall, N, *James III: a Political Study* (Edinburgh, 1982).

Macdougall, N, *James IV* (Edinburgh, 1989).

McGladdery, C A, *James II* (Edinburgh, 1990).

Reid, N H (ed.), *Scotland in the Reign of Alexander III, 1249–1286* (Edinburgh, 1990).

Wormald, J, *Mary Queen of Scots: a Study in Failure* (London, 1991).

Selective List of Sites to Visit

Monuments marked ★ are administered by Historic Scotland

Aberdeen
King's College Chapel, University of Aberdeen

Aberdeenshire
Drum Castle (National Trust for Scotland)

Angus
★Aberlemno Pictish Stones, Aberlemno
★Arbroath Abbey, Arbroath
★Brechin Cathedral and Round Tower, Brechin
★Restenneth Priory, Forfar
★St Vigean's Museum (collection of Pictish and early Scottish sculptured stones), Arbroath

Argyll
★Dunadd, Crinan
★Dunstaffnage Castle, Oban
Iona Abbey, Iona
★Rothesay Castle, Rothesay, Bute

Ayrshire
★Dundonald Castle, Dundonald

Berwickshire
Coldingham Priory, Coldingham

Dumbartonshire
★Dumbarton Castle, Dumbarton

Dumfriesshire
★Caerlaverock Castle, Glencaple
★Lincluden Collegiate Church, Dumfries

East Lothian
Dunbar Castle and Battlefield, Dunbar
★Tantallon Castle, North Berwick

Edinburgh
★Edinburgh Castle
★Holyrood Abbey and the Palace of Holyroodhouse
Parliament Hall, Parliament Square
★St Triduana's Chapel, Restalrig

Fife
★Dunfermline Abbey, Dunfermline
Falkland Palace, Falkland (National Trust for Scotland)
★Ravenscraig Castle, Kirkcaldy
★St Andrews Cathedral-Priory and Castle, St Andrews
St Monan's Church, St Monance

Glasgow
★Glasgow Cathedral

Inverness-shire
★Inverlochy Castle, Fort William

Kincardineshire
Kincardine Castle and King's Deer Park, Fettercairn

Kinross-shire
★Loch Leven Castle, Kinross

Kirkcudbrightshire
★Threave Castle, Castle Douglas

Moray
Burghead Fort, Burghead
★Duffus Castle, Duffus
 Pluscarden Abbey, Elgin
★Sueno's Stone, Forres

Perthshire
★Abernethy Round Tower, Abernethy
★Doune Castle, Doune
Dundurn, St Fillans
★Dunkeld Cathedral, Dunkeld
Dunsinnan Hill, Collace
★Huntingtower Castle, Perth
★Meigle Museum (collection of Pictish and early Scottish sculptured stones), Meigle
Scone Palace, Scone

Roxburghshire
★Hermitage Castle, Newcastleton
★Jedburgh Abbey, Jedburgh
★Kelso Abbey, Kelso
★Melrose Abbey, Melrose
Queen Mary's House, Jedburgh
Roxburgh Castle, nr Kelso

Renfrewshire
Paisley Abbey, Paisley

Ross-shire
Tain Collegiate Church and Chapels, Tain,

Stirlingshire
Bannockburn Battlefield, Bannockburn (National
    Trust for Scotland)
★Cambuskenneth Abbey, Stirling
★Inchmahome Abbey, Port of Menteith
★Stirling Castle, Stirling

West Lothian
★Linlithgow Palace, Linlithgow

Wigtonshire
★Whithorn Cathedral-Priory, Whithorn

There are also large collections of important royal
material in the National Museums of Scotland,
Edinburgh, and the National Portrait Gallery,
Edinburgh.

The Stationery Office

Published by The Stationery Office and available from:

The Stationery Office Bookshops

71 Lothian Road, Edinburgh EH3 9AZ (counter service only)

59-60 Holborn Viaduct, London EC1A 2FD
temporary location until mid-1998 (counter service only)

68–69 Bull Street, Birmingham B4 6AD Tel 0121–236 9696 Fax 0121–236 9699

33 Wine Street Bristol BS1 2BQ Tel 0117–926 4306 Fax 0117–929 4515

9–21 Princess Street, Manchester M60 8AS Tel 0161–834 7201 Fax 0161–833 0634

16 Arthur Street, Belfast BT1 4GD Tel 01232 238451 Fax 01232 235401

The Stationery Office Oriel Bookshop
The Friary, Cardiff CF1 4AA
Tel 01222 395548 Fax 01222 384347

The Stationery Office publications are also available from:

The Publications Centre (mail, telephone and fax orders only)

PO Box 276 London SW8 5DT
General enquiries 0171–873 0011
Telephone orders 0171–873 9090
Fax orders 0171–873 8200

Accredited Agents

(see Yellow Pages) and through good booksellers

Printed in Scotland for The Stationery Office Limited
J28291, C30, 10/97, CCN 056901.